TREEHOUSES

PAULA HENDERSON & ADAM MORNEMENT

TREEHOUSES

FRANCES LINCOLN

AB		MM	
MA		MN	
MB		MO	
MC		MR	
MD		MT	
ME		MW	
MG			
MH			

CONTENTS

INTRODUCTION

Early man, like his simian cousins, built houses in trees for his own safety. This practice continues today in some societies – notably in parts of Indonesia – where dangers on the ground, including bellicose neighbours, ferocious animals and flooding or other natural hazards, make more conventional earthbound dwellings impractical. Large trees have also been used to build elevated platforms, sometimes used by hunters as leafy 'hides', where they can wait unobserved until prey comes within easy range.

In these instances, treehouses have served as habitats for survival, but at least since Roman times, they have had another quite different role as places of pleasure and delight. The building of treehouses in private gardens and parks has brought fame, frivolity and fun to a previously strictly practical architectural form. What is more, the building of treehouses flourishes today as never before – some with access at dizzying heights via water-powered pulleys, others as large as a good-sized house and many constructed of the latest high-tec materials. Far from being constricted by necessity, today's young architects are daring to create treetop escapes that are not only beautiful and exciting, but imaginative and, at times, at the forefront of architectural experiment.

Treehouses are often built for children, as one would expect, but many others are built for more sophisticated pleasures and intellectual pursuits, and it is these which link the modern fascination with treehouses to their long history. For, as astonishing as many of these modern treehouses are, earlier treehouses were no less ambitious or imaginative. We know this from accounts and pictures by contemporary writers and artists, who recorded, often with great amazement, the treehouses they had seen or heard about. Unfortunately very few of these historic treehouses survive, for the treehouse is the most ephemeral of buildings. Yet, for centuries in both East and West, treehouses were built for a variety of purposes and in all sorts of shapes.

In the West, at least four 'golden ages' or major periods of treehouse building can be identified: ancient Roman times; Renaissance Europe; the Romantic period of the late eighteenth and early nineteenth centuries; and, again, our own day. We know less about the evolution of the treehouse in the East, only because descriptions of them are not as accessible. Paintings, drawings and prints, however, show that treehouses were built for important patrons and the forms they took sometimes expressed a different approach to nature than that of the West.

Treehouses of the past should amaze and amuse the readers of this book, just as they did the artists and writers who recorded them through the centuries. Equally, the quite spectacular treehouses of recent years, shown in numerous photographs and described in great detail, will also excite and inspire. What links them all together is passion: the passion of the architect and of the patron. The architect takes on the challenge of building high above ground, usually into a living organism – ever changing and sometimes frustratingly fragile. The patron envisages a treetop retreat, perhaps for his children, but just as likely for his own multifarious pleasures. That building and visiting a treehouse may involve some danger adds *frisson* to that passion. Treehouses are far more than simple hideaways. Read on and see ...

LEFT Treehouse of the Koyari people, near Port Moresby, New Guinea (c.1880)

Detail of a sixteenth-century English table carpet showing a naked man (wild man), chased by a savage lion, climbing up to his treetop refuge.

PAULA HENDERSON

TREEHOUSES OF THE PAST

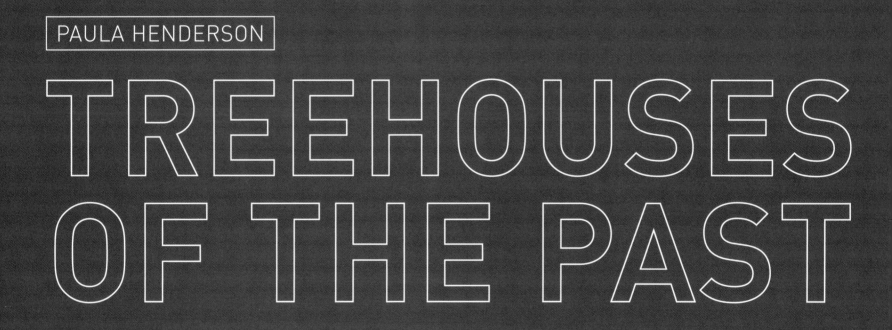

TREEHOUSES OF THE PAST

The idea of creating architecture from living materials dates back at least to the ancient Egyptians. They built retreats of vine-covered trellis to give much needed shade in the torrid desert climate and painted splendid *trompe-l'oeil* arbours or bowers in their tombs to provide a symbolic pleasurable setting, where the dead could enjoy the jars of wine and food that had been supplied for their use in the afterlife. Later, in the seventh century BC, the Assyrians showed similar scenes in their elegant bas-reliefs. In one, from the king's private apartments in the palace at Nineveh, King Ashurbanipal stretches out on an elegantly carved bench, sipping wine from a bowl, sheltered from the relentless Mesopotamian sun by a vine stretched between two trees. He is accompanied by his wife, seated nearby, and by servants, who fan the royal couple with palm branches. To the far left, the severed head of Teumman, King of Elam, dangles from the branch of another tree, a reminder of Ashurbanipal's recent military triumphs (1).

Gloating over vanquished enemies is not one of the pleasures normally associated with the arbour. Architecture made of natural materials is more often associated with sensuous pleasures: providing protection from the heat of the sun or the damp of rain. The arbour can also be fragrant when covered with roses, jasmine, honeysuckle or other sweet-smelling climbers. Flowers please the eye and any fruit can be plucked off and eaten. Birds and bees flutter and buzz about and cages can be hidden in the foliage so that the songs of the entrapped birds can be heard from within. The pleasure of sight can be enhanced by cutting windows into the foliage, so that the visitor can peer into the garden. Even better, the arbour can be erected high in the branches of a tree to provide a more spectacular prospect. This may well be how treehouses used for pure pleasure, rather than for defence, evolved from the simple earth-bound arbour. Exactly when this first happened is not known, but the earliest documented evidence dates from the first century AD.

In his *Natural History* (Book XII, chapter v), Pliny the Elder wrote of two treehouses, both built in great plane trees. One of these was erected by the notorious emperor Caligula on his estate in Velitrae, and there he 'held a banquet in the tree . . . in a dining room large enough to hold fifteen guests and the necessary servants', who also serenaded the group. Caligula referred to this as his 'nest', and Pliny could not resist adding cattily that the portly Caligula must have 'constituted a considerable portion of the shadow' cast by the tree that day.

The other treehouse described by Pliny was in Lycia. Rather than being built on the broad branches of the tree, the chamber was within a hollow cavity in the trunk, 'a cave of 81 foot in compasse'. This was 'so worthy to be deemed a marvel', Pliny wrote, that Licinius Mucianus (consul and lieutenant general of the province), 'held a banquet with eighteen members of his retinue inside the tree'. There he could 'sit secured from danger of wind . . . to heare the showers of rain to pat drop by drop, and rattle over his head upon the leaves'. Pliny wrote that Licinius enjoyed himself more among the foliage than he would have 'amid the resplendence of marble, painted decorations, tapestries and gilded panelling'. In his two accounts of these very early treehouses, Pliny has not only described two of the most common forms – the platform in the tree and the room within a hollow trunk – but also associated the treehouse with feasting and music. In the last quote, he also expressed the sublime paradox of the treehouse: man is both protected by and made more vulnerable to the vicissitudes of nature. Treehouses may be enjoyable, but the experience is enhanced by that *frisson* of risk.

Pliny was one of the most esteemed writers of antiquity and his accounts gave treehouses their classical pedigree, which may help to explain the sudden burst of enthusiasm for the form over a thousand years later in Renaissance Europe. Inspiration may also have come from a remarkable contemporary book, the *Hypnerotomachia Poliphili*, published first in Venice in 1499. Attributed to the Dominican monk, Francesco Colonna, the book told the story of young Poliphilus, who sought the beautiful nymph Polia. Beginning in a wilderness, he passed through wonderful landscapes filled with imaginative classical architecture. At one point he found himself in an enclosure, surrounded by large intertwined fruit trees. This 'most sweet and pleasant verdure . . . breathing foorth a most delectable and sweete odour' consisted of boughs of 'interstitous thicknes, the bowghes (not without a wonderful woorke) were so artificially twisted and growne together, that you might assend up by them, and not bee seene in them, nor yet the way where you went up' (2). Like Pliny, the author of the *Hypnerotomachia Poliphili* captured the magic of the treehouse. He also gave it a humanist, literary connection. The book, which was widely read and later translated into both French and English, must have influenced the great patrons of the sixteenth century. Among the most important of these were the immensely wealthy Medici family, whose treehouses in the gardens of their villas near Florence became tourist attractions and were among the first to be depicted by artists. The treehouse built by Cosimo I at Castello, for example, was described by both the Frenchman Michel de Montaigne (who saw it in 1580) and by the Englishman Fynes Moryson (who visited in 1594). Both particularly admired the 'water music' that played from hidden sources within the tree, but the fullest account was given by Giorgio Vasari in his life of the sculptor Niccolò il Tribolo:

> In a meadow to the east of the garden Tribolo planted a holm [oak] so thickly covered with ivy that it looked like a thicket, and it was approached by convenient wooden steps, at the top of which is a resting-place, with seats about it with backs, all of living green, and in the middle a marble table with a vase of variegated marble, into which water is brought by a pipe which spouts in the air . . . It is impossible to describe how the water is carried along the branches of this tree, to sprinkle people and to make fearful hissing sounds.

In 1599, the Flemish artist Giusto (or Justus) Utens was called upon to record the most famous of the Medici gardens, including Castello and *Il giardino delle meraviglie* (the garden of marvels) at Pratolino, which had been created for Cosimo's son, Francesco I, in the 1570s and 1580s (6). Filled with splendid fountains, automata and other works of art, the garden at Pratolino covered the hillside beneath the villa. At the very bottom of the garden, near the statue-covered 'Mount Parnassus', stood *La Fontana della Rovere* (the fountain of the oak). Utens showed a staircase curving around the trunk of the tree and disappearing into the abundant foliage (7). The staircase and platform were recorded

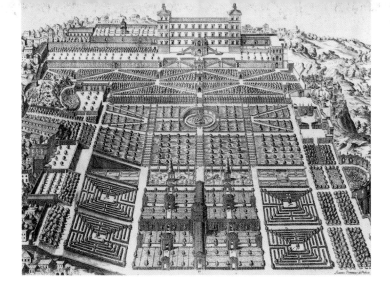

even more clearly in the later engraving by Stefano della Bella, who also showed the great octagonal enclosure surrounding the tree, with jets of water at each of the angles (3). In the engraving – and in a drawing by Giovanni Guerra – it is clear that there was not just a single stair but two stairs, each winding up and around the wide trunk of the tree. What is more, the stairs were not proper steps but broad ramps with branches looped back and forth to help secure footwork. Among the early documents associated with the garden at Pratolino are building accounts that include records of payment in 1582 to 'Brando legnaiolo' (Brando, the carpenter) for a model of these elaborate rustic stairs and another payment in the following year for their completion.

At the top of the tree was a platform, shown balustraded in Guerra's drawing, which we know from accounts was approximately eight metres in diameter and had *lochi da sedere* (places to sit) with a table from which spouted a *chiarissimo* (most clear) fountain. Agostino del Riccio wrote that when the fountain played visitors to the platform were showered with water as if standing in a heavy rain. In addition to these pleasures, visitors to the treehouse had panoramic views of the city of Florence and the lush valley of the Arno. Sadly, less than a century later, the tree was damaged in a storm and, along with its treehouse, had to be pulled down.

The fate of another, less celebrated, treehouse at Pratolino is not known, but it is also shown in Utens's view, just at the top of the cascade (8). This treehouse was built in an entirely different way. Instead of being supported on the large branches of an ancient oak, the platform was held up by posts with a slender tree growing through the centre offering skeletal support. The top branches of the tree were clipped into decorative clumps, forming a cheerful leafy finial. Something similar is visible in Utens's painting of the Medici villa at Caffagiolo and in even earlier views of the Villa d'Este in Tivoli, the hilltop retreat to the east of Rome that had been favoured by ancient Romans and was fashionable again in the sixteenth century. There, in the 1560s, Cardinal Ippolito II d'Este had created, with the help of the antiquarian

Pirro Ligorio, one of the most celebrated Renaissance gardens, captured in an engraving by the French architect Etienne Dupérac in 1573 (4). The primary entrance into the garden was through a large portal in the ancient wall at the bottom of the garden. From there the axial route to the villa began in a large square compartment, dominated and divided by long tunnel arbours. At the centre of that garden, where the arbours crossed, was a tall, multi-storey octagonal bower, supported by a tree at the centre. Again, the branches were bent to provide a screen and clipped to form decorative flourishes at the top (5).

Both forms of treehouse were recorded in other gardens, particularly in northern Europe, where the practice of building treetop retreats was taken up with gusto. The British traveller Thomas Coryate, for example, described the gardens of the Tuileries in Paris and wrote of 'two walkes . . . of equall length, each being 700 paces long, whereof one is so artificially roofed over with timber worke, that the boughes of the maple trees, wherewith the walke is on both sides beset ... cover it cleane over'. As at the Villa d'Este, the roofed walk had 'six faire arbours advanced to a great height like turrets'. In 1592 Fynes Moryson wrote that in the Swiss village of Shaffhausen he saw a 'Lynden . . . tree, giving so large a shade, as upon the top it hath a kinde of chamber, boarded on the floore, with windowes on the sides, and a cocke, which being turned, water falls into a vessel through divers pipes, by which it is conveyed thither for washing of glasses and other uses'. Here, in Protestant Europe, the spouts of water were not used to drench unwary passers-by, but for more sober, practical purposes.

The most wonderful depictions of Renaissance treehouses are found in Dutch and Flemish prints, published for a wide audience throughout Europe. Some prints were primarily architectural; others had more didactic, moralistic purposes. In both, treehouses played a role. The well-known Dutch painter and architect Hans Vredeman de Vries (1526–1609), for example, published a number of inventive and influential architectural treatises in the late sixteenth century, which presented classical

PRATOLINO

5 | PREVIOUS PAGE A fresco in the Villa d'Este, Tivoli, showing the gardens, including the multistorey bower, and pergolas in the lower garden.

6 | LEFT Giusto Utens's splendid lunette of 1599 recorded the Medici villa and gardens at Pratolino, including the two treehouses picked out here in the details: one (7) is towards the bottom and the other (8) is at the top of the cascade in the upper left of the painting.

7 | TOP Detail of the *Fontana della Rovere* at Pratolino, showing the lower treehouse.

8 | ABOVE Detail showing the upper treehouse, erected around a slender tree used for skeletal support, a type that became increasingly fashionable, particularly in northern Europe.

design in a highly imaginative and mannered way. His theoretical books on perspective and architectural forms often included wildly exaggerated views of buildings and their surrounding courts and gardens. One of his books, *Hortorum viridariorumque elegantes . . . formae*, published first in Antwerp in 1582 with many subsequent editions, included engravings of gardens in each of the classical orders (9). In these views, tunnel arbours were used to emphasize and define the geometric axes of the garden, as they had been at the Villa d'Este, and multi-storey arbours or treehouses were introduced at crucial intersections. These provided vertical accents to the garden, but one also suspects that Vredeman saw them as a suitable natural equivalent to the extravagant buildings shown in the background.

Vredeman, like many other northern European artists and architects, was clearly intrigued by arbours of all types. In a delicate tinted drawing of an unidentified garden, the tunnel arbours themselves are raised up, forming an elevated enclosed passageway, again with window-like openings and even little projecting balconies for viewing the garden and surrounding landscape (12). In a plate from his *Variae Architecturae Formae* (1601), four hermaphroditic herms support a square treehouse. As usual, a tree rises through the centre, bursting forth from the roof with tufts of greenery. In the background, long tunnel arbours with tall bowers stretch into the far distance (10).

One is tempted to dismiss such representations as the wild imaginings of a very creative artist, but other prints by contemporaries of Vredeman de Vries suggest that, impractical as they may seem, these structures must have been quite common. In engravings by Hans Bol, for example, treehouses are shown cantilevered out from the trunks of large trees and linked to houses by elevated, covered bridges. Similar treehouses became the centrepiece of May Day ceremonies, with villagers dancing and playing music beneath them (11).

In a number of allegorical prints – some with figures of Venus or of young lovers – large, multi-storey treehouses are shown in the background with lively figures feasting and dancing on different

Treehouses of the Past

12 | Hans Vredeman
de Vries's delightful
drawing of a garden
with an elevated
platform with bowers
and balconies, c.1570.

Bruegel. inuet.

13 | *Spring,* an engraving by Hieronymus Cock after Pieter Brueghel, illustrates the labours associated with the season, including work on a pergola. In the background, young men and women enjoy the pleasures of a treehouse.

levels. These prints may have been influenced by Pieter Brueghel's well-known painting of *Spring,* part of a series depicting the seasons that was subsequently issued in engravings published by Hieronymus Cock in 1570 (13). In the foreground, male and female gardeners rigorously hoe, dig and prepare beds for planting, while others struggle to tie vines on to the trellis of a pergola. Meanwhile, in the background a group of young dandies dance on the upper level of a treehouse, while below amorous couples feast and rest, listening to the music of a lone cellist. Implicit in such works is the contrast between diligent labourers and idle, irresponsible youth, and it seems likely that, to Brueghel at least, treehouses represented. élitist folly.

This is borne out in Brueghel's allegorical prints. In the series *The Seven Deadly Sins* (1556–58), he created a treehouse out of an open mussel shell, in imitation of his predecessor, Hieronymus Bosch, whose most bizarre treehouse was made from the body of a giant (14 and 15). Frequently in these works of art treehouses are prominent places for bad behaviour, not just by misbehaving youth, but also by clerics and monks. Although it may seem strange to put clerics in trees, there is evidence that medieval monks did study and pray in treetop retreats: one fifteenth-century miniature shows a monk sitting in a treehouse in a pear tree. If treetop 'hermitages' for clerics were common, they would have been a useful symbol for reforming, anti-clerical Protestants like Brueghel.

Dutch and Flemish prints were popular throughout Europe and it may have been an engraving that inspired the English painter, Robert Peake, when in 1603 he was called upon to make a portrait of the daughter of James I, the Princess Elizabeth, future Queen of Bohemia (16). The seven-year-old princess was depicted in a park with hunting scenes in the distance. Behind her is a familiar double-storey treehouse, but instead of crowds of frolicking youth, two young women sit quietly alone on a wattle seat that surrounds the base of the central supporting tree. Unlike those of Dutch prints, the treehouse is at the top of a snail mount, a feature far more common to English gardens than to those of

LVXVRIA ENERVAT VIRES, EFFOEMINAT ARTVS.

Luxurÿe stinckt / sÿ is vol onsuuerheden Sÿ breeckt die Crachten / en sÿ swackt die leden

14 | LEFT In his depiction of *Hell*, part of a triptych representing the *Garden of Earthly Delights* (c.1510), Hieronymus Bosch created a treehouse from part of a human body, just one of the many startling and enigmatic objects in the painting.

15 | ABOVE Pieter Brueghel was an admirer of Bosch. In this depiction of *Lust*, part of his series on *The Seven Deadly Sins* (1556–58), Brueghel used a mussel shell for a treehouse.

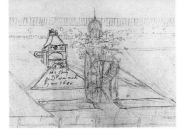

16 | LEFT In the background of his portrait of Elizabeth of Bohemia (1603), Robert Peake showed a mount with a treehouse at the top. Snail mounts with paths winding upward were common in grand English gardens of the period.

17 | TOP A treehouse built by John Evelyn in the garden of the family estate at Wotton, in Surrey, is shown here in a sketch he made in 1640. The treehouse was a perfect place for 'solitude' and 'retirement'.

18 | CENTRE The treetop chamber at Pishobury, as illustrated in Henry Chauncy's *Antiquities of Hertfordshire* in 1700.

19 | BOTTOM Detail of an estate map of Dothill, Shropshire, dated 1626, showing two domed bowers, each pierced by windows built into the branches of a single large tree.

the flat Lowlands. The painting has also lost any didactic message and, most important, has brought us to English gardens, some of which already included treehouses.

In the late sixteenth century, a magnificent multi-storied treehouse had been erected at Cobham Hall by Sir William Brook, Lord Cobham, described in great detail later by John Parkinson in *Paradisi in Sole, Paradisus Terrestris* (1629):

> And I have seene at Cobham in Kent, a tall or great bodied Line [lime] tree, bare without boughes for eight foote high, and then the branches were spread round about so orderly, as if it were done by art, and brought to compasse that middle Arbour: And from those boughes the body was bare againe for eight or nine foote (wherein might bee placed halfe an hundred men at the least, as there might be likewise in that underneath this) & then another rowe of branches to encompasse a third Arbour, with stayres made for the purpose to this and that underneath it: upon the boughes were laid boards to tread upon, which was the goodliest spectacle mine eye ever beheld for one tree to carry.

The treehouse at Cobham disappeared without trace, but a number of seventeenth-century examples were recorded in drawings, engravings and, as we have seen, paintings. A drawing by John Evelyn, for example, records the 'study & pond . . . made by me' for Wotton House in Surrey, the home of his elder brother (17). Beside the study is a treehouse, approached by a stairway that winds around the trunk of the tree to a platform hidden among the leafy branches, above which rises a charming little domed turret or outlook chamber. In 1643 Evelyn wrote in his diary that he 'built (by my Brothers permission) a study, made a fishpond, Iland and some other solitudes & retirements at Wotton, which gave the first occasion of improving them'. Evelyn would return again to Wotton in the 1650s, when he made even more alterations to the gardens, although it is not known whether the treehouse survived these or even the violent storms of 1649 that he recorded in his diary.

Estate maps and county histories show other early treehouses in England: one in a map of 1626 of Dothill in Shropshire and another at Pishobury, illustrated in Henry Chauncy's *The Historical Antiquities of Hertfordshire* (first published in 1700) (18 and 19). There must have been many more but only one early treehouse survives: the treehouse at Pitchford Hall in Shropshire, arguably the oldest treehouse in the world (20). Pitchford Hall, the home of the Ottley family from the fifteenth century, was enlarged in the seventeenth century and it seems likely that the treehouse would have been added to the gardens then. The first record of it is in a bird's-eye view of the house, signed by John Boiven in 1714. Approached by a wooden stair, the square house (approximately two and a half metres across) sits on the great horizontal branches of an ancient broad-leaved lime. Its survival may be attributed to the eighteenth-century owners of the Hall who brought in plasterers to 'modernise' and update it, rather than pulling it down. The

20 | The seventeenth-century treehouse at Pitchford Hall, Shropshire, possibly the oldest extant example in the world. Like the house, the treehouse is timber-framed and painted white. The ogee windows were added in the eighteenth century, when the interior was remodelled as well.

window and door openings were reset with rippling ogee heads and the interior plasterwork was embellished with charming 'rococo-gothick' motifs: clustered columns in the corners; a mask and sunburst at the centre and a pointed arcade running along the cornice with bow-knots at the springing of each arch. Although the broad-leaved lime can live to be over a thousand years old, the stresses of supporting the treehouse at Pitchford meant that recent owners have had to put steel reinforcements into the trunk of the tree. By doing this, they have saved both the tree and treehouse, now, quite rightly, declared a Grade I listed historic building.

Not all treehouses were found in private gardens. In 1653 Wenceslaus Hollar recorded the famous Hollow Tree in Hampstead, in what was meant to be a broadsheet advertisement for it (21). Hollar showed the impressive tree with figures entering into the narrow doorway that led to the spiral stair carved into the trunk, somehow without damaging the tree, judging by the luxurious growth of foliage. At the top, a platform holds a number of visitors, some seated on benches around the side. In his careful notes to the etching, Hollar wrote that there was room for six to sit and for another fourteen to stand. Hollow oak trees are mentioned at various other times in English history as well; some have become legendary. Robin Hood and his 'merry band of men' lived in a great oak tree in Sherwood Forest, which supposedly still stands. Like the Hampstead 'hollow tree', it was (and still is) a tourist attraction.

In 1697 Celia Fiennes visited Woburn Abbey, the Duke of Bedford's house in Bedfordshire, and admired the hunting park and gardens, which were typically formal with topiaried trees cut in the shape of 'beasts', neatly clipped arbours and a 'seate up in a high tree that ascends from the green 50 steps, that commands the whole parke round to see the Deer hunted, as also a large prospect of the Country'. As at Pishobury and Pitchford, this is rare evidence of the survival of a treehouse into the eighteenth century when it appears that they went out of favour. There may have been something too artificial about treehouses in the supposedly more 'natural' English landscape garden. Instead of being 'curious' or 'witty', garden architecture had a certain *gravitas*, reminiscent of the 'golden age' of antiquity. Classical gates, pyramids and, especially, temples were considered far more appropriate to these pastoral landscapes. Furthermore, the great success of the English landscape garden spelled the doom of many earlier gardens and their treehouses. Even far-away Pratolino was not exempt – it was eventually stripped of its many wonders and transformed into a bland grassy field.

In the mid-eighteenth century, Sir William Chambers produced drawings and engravings of an almost endless variety of garden buildings for Princess Augusta at Kew, including an 'Alhambra' and the famous, still standing 'Chinese Pagoda'. Yet, the only architect producing anything like a treehouse was the astronomer and polymath, Thomas Wright of Durham. Wright's *Universal Architecture*, published in 1755, contained a book devoted to 'Six Original Designs of Arbours', including retreats for a druid or hermit, an aviary and a building for a 'wilderness'. All were constructed of natural materials, including living trees and gnarled knotty pieces of wood. If none of these little buildings was a true treehouse, Wright noted that none was 'to appear in Sight of another or of any regular Piece of Architecture, being imagined to please most, where they may be naturally supposed the only Productions of the Age, before Building became a Science'. In other words, these buildings were to look primitive and rustic, as if built before the development of true architecture.

The ideas expressed by Wright foreshadowed the new ideas about nature that would develop later in the century, when romanticism and an appreciation of the sublime would result in another 'golden age' of treehouse building, one that would rival even that of the sixteenth and seventeenth centuries. Suddenly, raw nature was praised, valued above the artificial pastoral landscapes of 'Capability' Brown and his followers. Similarly, 'primitive man' or 'the noble savage' was seen as superior to those corrupted by western culture and society. This prehistoric, pre-architectural, pre-societal man, had, of course, lived in

21 | Wenceslaus Hollar's etching of the Hollow Tree in Hampstead. This tree had a spiral stair in the trunk leading to the spacious platform at the top of the tree.

1. The Bottom aboue ground in Compaſs is —— 28. foote
2. The Breadth of the doore is —— 2. foote
3. The Compaſs of the Turret on the Top is —— 34. foote
4. The Doore in Height to goe in is—6 foot. 2 Inches
8. The Height to the Turret is —— 33. foote
11. The Lights into the Tree is —— ·16
18. The Stepps to goe vp is —— 42
19. The Seat aboue the Stepps,

Six may Sitt on, and round about roome for foureteene more
All the way you goe vp within the Hollow Tree ——·.

22 | Although treehouses were not a feature of eighteenth-century gardens, a painting by Anthony Devis depicting 'The Man in the Moon Inn', suggests that one may have served as a pub in the 1770s.

Notre établissement dans l'arbre (page 44).

11. ROBINSON — Le Vrai arbre

P. Javelle, phot., Robinson

treehouses, or so it was believed. If the great philosopher of the movement was Jean-Jacques Rousseau, the impetus for building treehouses was advanced by the immensely popular novel, *Swiss Family Robinson*, written by Johann Rudolf Wyss in 1813. The virtuous Swiss family, left behind by the other passengers who crowded the lifeboats after their ship had been destroyed on a reef, created a life for themselves on a small island near New Guinea. For protection, they built their house in a tree. The superiority and godliness of this wholesome, if difficult, life caught the imagination of people then, as it continues to do now, judging by the number of times that the book has been reprinted, translated into almost every language and filmed for the cinema and television (23).

No one knows how many treehouses were built as a result of Wyss's book, but the most impressive progeny was Parc Robinson, created in the French village of Plessis, about eighteen miles from Paris. The park had been established late in the eighteenth century in the grounds of the Château de Sceaux. Some fifty years later, a young Parisian restaurateur, M. Gueusquin, visited the park with his wife and was struck by the great size and beauty of the chestnut trees. Encouraged by the popularity of *Robinsonnades*, Gueusquin envisioned a park full of treehouse retreats. His dreams became reality when he built Le Grand Robinson or Le Vrai Arbre, a restaurant high in the branches of one of the largest trees. There, *haute cuisine* was delivered to the diners in baskets raised by pulleys (24). Visitors could take their meal on any one of a number of different platforms, all of which were supported further by sturdy wooden stilts. Rustic balustrades were constructed around the sides to prevent anyone falling off. Before long, another treehouse was built across the road, Le Grand Arbre, even larger and more spectacular. When developers ran out of chestnut trees, they improvised: L'Arbre des Roches, so-called because of the grotto in its base, was constructed of concrete, shaped and formed to look like a tree. Surviving postcard views of Parc Robinson show the main street, Rue de Malabris, lined with little buildings for entertaining the

23 | LEFT The evocative descriptions and images of Johann Rudolf Wyss's *Swiss Family Robinson* have been an enduring inspiration: the illustration shown here is from a late nineteenth-century French edition.

24 | ABOVE The most ambitious venture into treehouse building was Parc Robinson, in the French village of Plessis, captured here in a contemporary postcard.

25 | BELOW L. Audot's treatise on garden ornament, originally published in 1819, included numerous examples of rustic, picturesque buildings, including this jolly, leafy treehouse.

26 | RIGHT Victor Petit's elegant garden pavilion appears to be a cross between a treehouse and a giant parasol. It was built in Parc de la Motte, Bourgogne. From *Habitations Champêtres* (c.1855).

throngs of people who came. By the early years of the twentieth century, Parc Robinson was the place to go, not only for dining, but for games, dancing, courting and weddings. One popular song celebrated the romantic reputation of the park.

> Do you remember, Lison, it was a Sunday bright
> I took you to Robinson dressed all in white
> There among the branches, what kisses, what delight . . .

Little survives today of Parc Robinson in the renamed village of Plessis-Robinson, apart from the Rue Malabris and a number of trees with fragments of platforms.

Just as travellers' descriptions and contemporary drawings

provide evidence of Renaissance treehouses, the books on garden design and architecture that proliferated in the nineteenth century demonstrate how widespread the 'picturesque' or *rustique* architecture of Parc Robinson was. In 1819, L. Audot published his *Traité de la composition et de l'ornament des jardins* (Treatise on the composition and ornament of gardens), a popular book that went into numerous editions and reprints. The first volume contained the explanatory text and the second, the plates: illustrations of delightful seats, espaliered arbours, pavilions, *fabriques d'ornément* (ornamental buildings), *portiques de la Gymnastique* (swing-sets) and kiosks of every description (25). Natural materials were used everywhere: roofs were thatched and walls were created of trellis and woven branches. Where nature was insufficient, man-made materials – cement and iron – were used to create some of the more bizarre structures. In 1855, Victor Petit published *Habitations Champêtres – Recueil de Maisons, Villas, Chalets, Pavillons, Kiosques, Berceaux, Parterres, gazons, serres, orangeries, parcs et jardins* – which included slightly less eccentric, more buildable rustic seats and treehouses (26).

The great interest in treehouses that was epitomized by an entire park outside Paris devoted to them continued into the twentieth century, initially on a less spectacular scale. The architect and garden designer Harold Peto, best known for his devotion to the Italian formal garden, designed a treehouse for Daisy, Countess of Warwick, at Easton Lodge, Essex, in 1902 (27, 28 and page 10). Not surprisingly, the treehouse, which could seat up to ten adults, was called 'Le Robinson'. Its thatched roof and wattle walls could have come right out of Audot's treatise, as could the rather grander treehouse built at the same time by Sir Thomas Lipton at his home in Enfield (29).

In 1914, an American, Phebe Westcott Humphreys, published *The Practical Book of Garden Architecture*. The twelfth chapter was devoted to 'Crows'-Nests and Tree Houses: secluded retreats ideal for securing rest and inspiration', perhaps the first practical guide to building treehouses. Crows'-nests were basically viewing platforms, so needed no roof other than the green foliage of the

26 & 27 | Harold Peto's charming thatched treetop chamber was erected for the Countess of Warwick at Easton Lodge in 1902 and called 'le Robinson'. The treehouse survives in part and Peto's original drawing will form the basis of any restoration.

tree. Her advice was sensible and fairly obvious: treehouses should be built of materials that would not be harmed by weather and floors were to be laid evenly on the branches of the tree, supported on 'strong posts embedded in the ground'. 'Winding rustic stairs' provided access and could be converted into 'objects of beauty' by planting climbers (she suggested wisteria) up the posts. She wisely advised, too, that the railings around the platform must be 'fall-proof'.

Although a proper treehouse might require an architect, Humphreys advised that 'almost any handy man should be able to design and build a satisfactory structure'. The illustrations in her book suggest that architects were not involved, yet these slightly haphazard structures are probably representative of a large percentage of treehouses built in the twentieth century by children or their eager fathers. For Humphreys, treehouses were not meant to be an ornamental feature of the garden, but to provide 'delightful seclusion up among the breezes in a shelter of tree branches'. They could be used as a work room for an author, artist or for those composing music, who would be inspired by the 'bird songs caroled in the upper branches'. Humphreys's own inspiration to create a writing room in the branches of a tree adjoining her 'den' had been a description of a writers' colony in the Catskill Mountains, where treehouses were built 'among the trees' rather than 'in a tree'. The advice in Humphreys's book was sound and, equally important, she captured the enduring spirit of the treehouse when she wrote that 'the harmony of the structure with its surroundings will be a source of unending satisfaction'.

If the history of the treehouse in the West can be traced back to Roman precedents, it is more difficult to provide a continuous history of the treehouse in the East, where the cultures were so much more diverse and the evidence so elusive. In many of the oriental religions, certain types of trees were revered, considered sacred ground. Trees were planted with care and precision in gardens, often in the four cardinal directions, to 'evoke the presence of the Four Guardian Gods', so building a pleasure pavilion in a tree might have been deemed disrespectful.

29 | A tea party in the treehouse at Ossidge, Enfield; an appropriate entertainment for Sir Thomas Lipton (photograph *c.* 1900).

The essence of Chinese and Japanese gardens was that they attempted to recreate on a small scale the spiritual character of nature as a whole. Architecture within gardens was meant to provide a place to study and contemplate nature, epitomized by the little, rustic hermitages (or *t'ings*) one finds in paintings of even the remotest landscapes. A *t'ing* in the wilderness was meant to demonstrate man's relatively minor place in the natural order. Buildings erected within gardens took on a more emphatic presence, often brightly coloured and almost always with fantastic roofs that curled up in the corners. Treehouses seem to have played no role.

In Japan, 'moon-watching pavilions', all built according to predetermined measurements and with precise numbers of components, were placed in optimum positions to gaze at the moon and its reflection. Viewing other aspects of nature was also considered important and, in one case, required an elevated vantage point. The Tsuten garden in Kyoto was famed for its collection of wild maple trees, which produced the most spectacular display of autumn colour. Elevated walks and platforms were erected specifically so that visitors could admire the leaves from above (30).

Although the representation of man was normally forbidden in Islamic art, both Persian and Mughal artists were permitted to capture the magnificent and highly sensuous world of great kings, princes and noblemen. Gardens were among the most important pleasure grounds and often contained splendid open pavilions and treehouses. Typically, a number of miniatures show handsome young men and beautiful courtesans enjoying themselves in their lofty 'love nests' (31). In other miniatures, these arboreal retreats were used for more intellectual activities. The great Mughal emperor Akbar, who ruled from 1556 to 1605, for example, was never taught to read. His father and tutors knew that there would always be a wise man or poet only too willing to recite his works to the king. The poetry of the twelfth-century Persian poet, Anvari, was among his favourites and in 1588 a small book was produced for the king that included a miniature showing Anvari reciting his

30 | ABOVE Elevated walkways were erected in the Tsuten Garden in Kyoto, Japan, to enable visitors to look down on the glowing colours of autumn foliage.

31 | RIGHT An early-sixteenth-century Persian miniature depicting *The garden of the fairies*.

32 | **LEFT** The revered poet Anvari entertains a young prince in his elevated summer-house. A Mughal miniature attributed to the artist Basawan and made for the emperor Akbar the Great in 1588.

33 | **OVER PAGE** 'Monkey Town' from *Zephir the Monkey*, one of Jean de Brunhoff's wonderful and imaginative tales of Babar the Elephant.

work to a young prince, who raises his cup of wine to salute the sage. The two sit on a fine carpet in a beautiful open platform, ornamented with inlaid mosaic decoration (32). Below them, servants busily prepare food and drink to bring up the ladder to the two men. In India these treehouses were usually built in chenar trees which, like the oaks and plane trees in western gardens, seemed to be able to withstand the weight and disruption. As in the west, almost nothing survives of these fine pleasure pavilions.

Although the dominant thought today is that treehouses are perfect playhouses for children, historically in both East and West these arboreal constructions were built for adults. Roman emperors saw them as places for dining and entertaining. The Medici did the same, adding witty *giochi d'acqua* or water tricks to surprise guests. In parts of northern Europe, treehouses took on even more ambitious forms, with elevated walkways or layered platforms, where young lovers danced and played. It is obvious that these little garden buildings had become perfect places for trysting, something that was given a slightly censorious twist in contemporary moralistic prints. Treehouses were also seen as havens for intellectual thought, artistic stimulation and spiritual reflection. An ancient oak tree in Allouville, near Le Havre in France, has been used as a chapel for many centuries. There is a small chamber at the top of a tree and another, set in the hollow trunk near the bottom, where a local priest still occasionally says mass (see pages 80–85).

Treehouses have also been associated with the 'primitive hut', the safe haven for early man. In the late eighteenth century this was equated with the 'noble savage', that admirable being who had not yet been corrupted by society or by its pretentious architecture. This connection appears even earlier, however, in the late-sixteenth-century Bradford Table Carpet, where a naked young man climbs up into his thatched treetop dwelling in order to escape from a charging lion (page 6). This scene appears twice and is to be contrasted with scenes along the longer side of the carpet of young dandies parading with their ladies in front of elaborate, domed houses. Although predating Rousseau by almost two hundred years, the lesson appears to be the same.

The celebration of the moral superiority of treetop living culminated, as we have seen, in the Romantic period with the novel *Swiss Family Robinson*, which provided inspiration for treehouses for at least a century and a half afterwards. The literary tradition was further revived in the twentieth century, especially in children's literature. Edgar Rice Burroughs's tales of Tarzan, the aristocratic English orphan raised in the African jungle by apes, is, in a way, a variation on the nobility of the primitive life of *Swiss Family Robinson*. Although Tarzan's treehouse is only a temporary refuge for him in the original book, published in 1914, the enduring memory for many people is of the filmed version with the athletic Johnny Weissmuller swinging on vines from tree to tree, howling his distinctive warnings to other animals, and arriving safely back to his treetop cabin.

Anthropomorphized animals, so common in children's literature, often lived in treehouses. In one of Jean de Brunhoff's many charming stories about Babar the Elephant, Babar's friend, Zephir the monkey, returned home during the summer holidays. His family lived in Monkey Town, which consisted of pretty little treehouses hanging on the branches of trees like ornaments on a Christmas tree, all reached by rope-ladders (33). Zephir's house had a thatched roof, green shutters and windows. Others had balconies, window boxes and chimneys. Perhaps inspired by the equally French Parc Robinson, there was a restaurant with 'marvellous views'.

One of the most beloved modern children's stories is *Winnie-the-Pooh* by A. A. Milne, where many of the characters, including the boy, Christopher Robin, had treehouses. Owl lived in The Chestnuts, 'an old-world residence of great charm, which was grander than anybody else's, or so it seemed to Bear, because it had both a knocker *and* a bell-pull' (35). In another great favourite, J. R. R. Tolkien's *Lord of the Rings*, the Hobbits live in underground burrows, while their allies, the Elves, live in fantastic dwellings in giant 'Mallorn' trees that soar frighteningly into the sky (34).

HAIRDRESSER

PALACE

MONKEYS

34 | **BELOW** The golden
Mallorn trees of
Lothlorien, home
of the Wood Elves in
J. R. R. Tolkien's *Lord
of the Rings*.

35 | **OPPOSITE** Winnie-
the-Pooh pauses
thoughtfully before
announcing his arrival
at Owl's house.

These are just a few of the many stories that feature treehouses and there can be little doubt that the children who read these books and saw them brought to life by creative film-makers were enchanted. Many, no doubt, were inspired to go home and build their own treehouses. In most cases, the result would have been a few boards nailed to the branches of trees, much like those described in Phebe Westcott Humphreys' *Practical Book*. Increasingly, though, treehouses are being built by grown men and women, still inspired by childhood stories but now with the funds to commission architects to fulfil their dreams. These architects are flexing their wings and making full use of modern technologies and high-tec materials, and as a result we are witnessing a splendid new golden age of treehouses. But for sheer invention and delight, there is still plenty to learn from Hans Vredeman de Vries, Mughal miniatures, the Swiss Family Robinson and even Jean de Brunhoff's swinging Monkey Town.

ADAM MORNEMENT

TREEHOUSES OF TODAY

TREEHOUSES OF TODAY

Treehouses promise escape. Where better to rise above the demands of daily life? Today, as well as traditional follies and play spaces, treehouses offer independence in the form of offices, artists' studios and hotel rooms.

Increased knowledge about tree maintenance, improved construction techniques and the viability of adding plumbing and power sources mean that there are now few functions a treehouse cannot perform. This section demonstrates the diversity of contemporary treehouses.

The search for privacy takes many forms. In some cultures, tree platforms are used as spiritual retreats, or hidden vantage points from which to watch over livestock. In others, they are used as childhood hideaways – a young John Lennon built one in his garden, overlooking Strawberry Fields.

Prokop Zavada, a Czech enthusiast, used his treehouse as a weekend getaway (see pages 120–21). Located deep within ancient woodland an hour's drive from Prague, Zavada built two simple platforms in separate trees, and linked them with cargo net to create an enormous hammock twenty metres up. Zavada's retreat was an escape from urban pressures, to be enjoyed by friends and family.

In terms of spirit and appearance, Zavada took inspiration from the British tree protestors of the mid-1990s (see pages 62–65), whose actions played a small but important role in forcing the British government to engage more closely with its electorate, particularly in matters of infrastructure planning.

Aside from protecting and getting back to nature, perhaps the most common reason for building a treehouse is delight. The prospect of defying gravity while immersed in the natural world seems to have universal appeal. At his private home in Provence, director and film star John Malkovich co-designed a series of play structures for his children, including a small wicker 'tree nest' woven into the branches of a walnut tree (see pages 116–19).

Not all treehouses are so elaborate. The majority are little more than a few planks of wood that last for a couple of summers. But the number of companies around the world specializing in treehouse construction suggests that interest is stronger than ever.

Such is the level of expertise that a treehouse can meet almost any challenge. In early 2005 the Alnwick Garden treehouse – thought to be the world's largest – opened in Northumberland. The vast network of pathways and activity spaces was commissioned by the Duchess of Northumberland as an addition to the public gardens at Alnwick Castle. It includes a 100-seat restaurant, gallery space, play decks and two large classrooms for school groups (see pages 108–113).

It is still rare for a treehouse to be a full-time residence, but aside from some planning regulations there are few prohibitive factors. One man who proves the point is Sam Edwards, resident of Calhoun in the Appalachian foothills of North Georgia (see pages 122–27). Since 1990 Edwards has lived in a treehouse composed largely of vehicular salvage – the nose cone of an abandoned jet is his bedroom.

That is another thing about treehouses, the people who have built them usually have quite a story to tell.

LEFT Bedroom at the Green Magic Treehouse Resort in Kerala, one of the growing number of treehouses to visit around the world.
PREVIOUS PAGE A Portaledge in use near Mendocino, California (see page 144).

TREEHOUSES OF NECESSITY

FRAGILE TRADITIONS

THE KOROWAI PEOPLE IRIAN JAYA, INDONESIA

Dutch missionary Johannes Veldhuizen made contact with the Korowai people of Irian Jaya on 4 October 1978. Deep in the rainforest of Indonesia's easternmost province he found an ancient warrior community of treehouse dwelling hunter-gatherers.

The existence of the Korowai's treehouses offers an insight into a lost South Sea tradition. Only a few hundred years ago forest-based communities in equatorial regions around the globe lived in similar structures, for similar reasons.

The houses are typically built 10–12 metres above the ground, although some reach as high as 35 metres. Visual delicacy belies structural strength – the nest-like treehouses often survive five years with minimal maintenance. And they are strong enough to accommodate families of eight to ten, including all possessions and livestock.

Korowai treehouses occupy ancestral territories. Two, sometimes three stand in jungle clearings. The treehouse has enormous significance to the Korowai, reflecting social hierarchies and spiritual beliefs.

Large treehouses have separate areas for men and women. The largest have separate stairs and entrances. Stairs are made of thin poles with notches cut as foot-holes. Rattan is used to tie the pole to the floor platform of the treehouse. Both the stairs and threshold beam are smeared with animal fat, to guarantee continuous welfare.

The fire occupies a central position in every treehouse. Occupants sleep around it and prepare food on it. To counter the threat of blaze the fireplace, a basket of wooden spars, is filled with a layer of leaves and clay and suspended in a hole with rattan. When a fire burns out of control the rattan is cut, and it falls to the ground.

When building a treehouse a large banian or wambon tree is selected as the pole. Working from temporary platforms the Korowai build the floor base, which is supported by between four and ten poles. Before they fix the supports, they fill the holes in which they will be inserted with leaves or grass stalks, to prevent demons entering the house.

The floor is composed of tightly packed thin wooden spars, covered with bark of the nibung or dal tree. Wall frames are made from the shafts of sago leaves. The leaves of the sago palm also form the roof, which consists of two wings at an angle of around 70 degrees. Sago trees are the Korowai's main source of trade and sustenance. The sago grub feast is the central ritual of community life.

Treehouses are home to the Korowai for a variety of reasons, practical and mystical. Irian Jaya is a densely forested island ripe with predators and tropical diseases. And the Korowai occupy a low-lying stretch of land between the Becking and Eillanden rivers where attacks and flood are constant hazards. On a more esoteric level the Korowai believe treehouses offer protection from sorcerers.

The Korowai, who may number only 3000 in total, are fiercely isolationist. In anthropological circles rumours abound of cannibalistic traditions and bloodthirsty feuds with the region's 250 indigenous tribes. What is certain are the Korowai's animist convictions, and their belief that all deaths are a consequence of witchcraft. As a culprit must always be found and killed the cycle of inter-tribe revenge killings is never-ending.

The future is uncertain for the Korowai and their ancient tree dwelling tradition. The Indonesian government regard Irian Jaya, their most recent and largest acquisition, as a well-stocked larder

PREVIOUS PAGE Korowai hunters pass the abandoned treehouse of Landi Gifanop in Irian Jaya. **LEFT** Visual delicacy belies structural strength – the treehouses often last for five years.

of natural resources. Irian Jaya became an Indonesian province in 1963, when the Dutch left their last East Indian colony. The local population had nothing in common with Indonesia's Asian, predominantly Muslim culture, but Indonesia's quest for new territory (named 'Victorious Hot Land') took precedence over ethnic harmony.

The area forms the western half of Papua New Guinea. It is home to a human population of just 1.9 million. Underneath the lucrative landscape of rain forest, snow capped peaks, and powerful rivers, are deposits of copper, gold and oil. The Indonesian government is exploiting Irian Jaya's resources and using it as a receptacle for human overspill – Indonesia is the world's fourth most populous country. It is a wilderness of opportunities. Native tribes will not be allowed to stand in the way of development.

To date a huge majority of Korowai have resisted integration into Indonesian culture. Despite more than two decades of concerted efforts, missionaries have failed to baptise a single tribe member. But others have not been so resilient.

It may be only a question of time before Korowai traditions are broken down. But for now they represent a link to a forgotten world.

LEFT The Korowai move naturally among the trees in which they live.

ABOVE Treehouse construction is a group activity.

LEFT AND RIGHT Fire occupies a central position in every treehouse.

DEFENDING NATURE

PROTEST TREEHOUSES UK AND USA

During the 1990s some of the world's most inventive treehouses were the product of direct action against developments deemed detrimental to the natural habitat. The British were particularly proactive in the field, but by no means unique.

Anti-road activists in Britain first used tree dwelling as a defensive strategy in July 1993, at Jesmond Dene, near Newcastle. In the eyes of protestors the Cradlewell Bypass was an unwelcome hangover of 1960s planning policy, an era when social and environmental issues were barely considered in new road developments. Of particular concern to the protestors was the culling of 180 mature trees and the loss of a public park.

The Flowerpot Tribe, a loose collective of anti-road activists, began to gather in the Jesmond Dene woodland from June 1993. Their intention was to delay clearance work. After a few weeks the tension spilled over into a fight, forcing some of the protestors into the trees. Necessity being the mother of invention, makeshift treehouses were erected overnight. The majority were hammocks with overhead tarpaulins for protection. For the next few months the tree sitters developed their homes and linked them together with ropes. Their efforts were not enough to save the trees, but a trend had been established.

Perhaps the most notorious British 'twigloo' community was built at Fairmile, Devon. In 1994 a thirteen mile by-pass was proposed between Honiton and Exeter. Activists believed that the road improvement scheme did not justify the loss of untouched woodland and countryside. Over the next two years the Fairmile Camp developed into a complex network of treehouses and tunnels. For a while Daniel Hooper, aka Swampy, was a household name in Britain.

The Fairmile camp was built in and around a copse of mature oaks, the largest of which was 400 years old. Residents called themselves the Quercus Tribe, after the Latin word for oak. Protestor and photographer Ingrid Crawford recalls a shallow trench and barricade of salvaged wood around the trees, as protection against approaching machinery. Visitors entered across a small bridge. Once inside they were confronted with a community of small treehouses, tunnels, benders and a caravan.

'Some of the treehouses were 25 metres,' says Crawford. 'There was even a boat tied up there, with a tarp slung over it. Apparently it was cosy and rocked in the breeze.' Access to the treehouses was not easy. It involved wearing a harness and climbing through the branches. Depending on the height of your treehouse, it might also require you to clamber through, or over other people's treehouses.

They were not sophisticated structures. In fact the majority were probably extremely dangerous. A typical 'twigloo' was made of a cargo net or hammock, ropes for a roof frame, and as much tarpaulin as could be tied down. The walkways were made of two ropes, one to attach your harness, the other to walk along.

LEFT At Fairmile protestors were evicted after a three-year occupation.

But in combination the treehouses made an impressive impact, reminiscent of the Ewoks' village in *Star Wars: Return of the Jedi* [see also pages 130–131]. At night Crawford remembers the treehouses glowing like large candles bouncing in the wind. And they were resilient. It was January 1997 before the camp was evicted.

When the end came, it was swift. Complacency meant that not all anti-road protestors were manning their positions when the police staged a dawn raid. A circle of yellow-jacketed policemen closed tight around the camp, stopping any new arrivals getting in. But removing the protestors was no easy task. Some had linked arms in tunnels, as a final gesture of defiance. 'It took all day to bring everybody down from the trees, and out of the tunnels', recalls Crawford. 'They came down miserably, but peacefully.'

Fairmile did not succeed in stopping the road development, but the protest did cause a substantial budgetary overrun. Estimates suggest that an effective camp can add £10 million to the cost of a road-building scheme. And the extensive media coverage of Fairmile helped convince the Conservative government that the British people were serious about their objection to large-scale road-building programmes.

All over the world the 1990s were halcyon days for tree protests. On 18 December 1999 in California, Julia 'Butterfly' Hill completed her 738-day vigil in a Californian redwood. Hill was protesting against the Pacific Lumber Company's plan to cut down a stretch of mature woodland in Humboldt County. It took over two years for a deal to be stuck, sparing the 600-year-old giant. Hill lived on two 1.8m x 1.8m platforms, 60 metres above the ground. She was visited by, among others, folk singer Joan Baez. She has since become the youngest person ever to be inducted into the Ecology Hall of Fame, and she generated an enormous amount of publicity.

A legacy of the 1990s tree protests is an institutional fear of potential costs and embarrassment. Today community engagement is a pre-requisite in any major development. In the rare instances of a government risking the activists' wrath, a swift compromise is a common outcome. In the summer of 2003 the British government backed down over plans for the Arundel by-pass in East Sussex. The decision came only a few days after two national newspapers revealed that tree protestors were preparing to occupy woodland along the proposed route.

Today the threat of a tree-sit is often enough to stop development. It might seem unlikely, but history will record that during the 1990s treehouses played a vital role in forcing governments to engage more closely with their electorates.

LEFT ABOVE
Protestors in the copse of oaks at Fairmile, Devon, UK.

LEFT BELOW
A treehouse improvised from a boat at Fairmile.

ABOVE RIGHT
Julia 'Butterfly' Hill during her 738-day occupation of a Californian redwood.

BELOW RIGHT
Hill lived on two platforms 60 metres above the ground.

GROWING HOMES

PROTOTYPE FAMILY HOUSE ADDIS ABABA, ETHIOPIA

The Ethiopian architect Ahadu Abaineh has a plan to tackle his country's urban housing crisis. Unfortunately he is having difficulty getting people to take it seriously.

In recent years growing rural poverty has placed increasing pressure on African cities. Addis Ababa is no exception. Steady population expansion has created a city with insufficient housing stock, intense pressure on ecological resources, and unsanitary living conditions, particularly in suburban areas.

Abaineh wants to address two of these problems in one hit, by mass-producing affordable family homes with living trees as corner posts. Fast-growing eucalyptus trees create the load-bearing structure, which is filled in with traditional mud walls – the mud is mixed with hay and trodden into pulp by cattle. A corrugated iron roof protects the walls and channels rain-water to the trees' roots.

As the family grows, so does the house. The first two prototype houses are two-storey dwellings, with the potential for the addition of a third level, depending on the health of the eucalyptus trees. One of the houses, belonging to a friend of Abaineh, accommodates him, his mother, his wife, and their two children.

The simple design is made of the earth; all materials are locally sourced and sustainable. And over the course of its life it gives something back to the earth – a well-maintained eucalyptus tree will live for 120 years. The trees help tackle pollution, and improve the appearance of the city.

Further benefits include the speed of construction: the prototype houses were built in only five weeks by a carpenter and two assistants. They are also a fraction of the cost of conventional houses. Abaineh estimates that a treehouse can be built for only twenty per cent of its steel and concrete equivalent, working out at about $US30 per square metre. This would be an important consideration anywhere, but particularly so in Ethiopia, a nation of extreme poverty. The materials and method of construction also help to demystify the process of creating shelter. 'This means there's no need for consultants and contractors to satisfy a basic human need,' says Abaineh.

He would like to build a group of ten houses. 'But it's difficult getting the land. I'm negotiating with the municipality, but they think the idea is a little weird.' Abaineh has also encountered a certain amount of public scepticism, particularly from neighbours. But he lives in hope. Groves of eucalyptus seedlings have been planted, which he hopes to nurture to maturity in anticipation of changing policy and attitudes.

TOP Simple wooden ladders give access between floors.

RIGHT Additional levels can be added depending on the health of the trees.

ABOVE Fast growing eucalyptus trees provide the load-bearing structure.

TREEHOUSES TO VISIT

ALONE IN THE WILD

WILDERNESS TREEHOUSE LODGE ALASKA, USA

Eric Schmidt's treehouse, in the foothills of the Alaskan range, is 90 miles from the nearest road. Black and grizzly bears are the immediate neighbours. It is one of the most isolated treehouses in the world. And for a cost of around US$900 it is available for hire for five nights, a price that includes Schmidt's services as a guide.

'The treehouse was an accident in its inception,' says Schmidt, a wilderness guide and owner of the Alaskan retreat. He moved from Colorado to Alaska in 1982 and throughout the 1980s this explorer and outdoor pursuits enthusiast spent his summers working as a fishing guide on an isolated lake deep in the Alaskan wilderness. After a while it occurred to him to cement his ties to the area. 'The obvious idea was do to a "homestead",' he explains.

Until 1990 the US government was still offering favourable land rights to people prepared to populate its wild north. The homestead arrangement required prospective tenants to find a site and build an insulated home with a door, window, heating and cooking stove. To seal the deal 'homesteaders' had to live on the property for 25 months over a five-year period, and have the property surveyed.

It took almost ten years of searching before Schmidt found a stretch of land that looked like home, but in early 1990 he happened upon a beautiful spot overlooking the Alaskan range.

His first job was to build a 'cache', an animal-proof elevated area, to store supplies for his return. 'I found a group of dead trees, pictured a platform between them, then looked at the placement of a live tree in the group, and envisioned a platform large enough for my tent. Soon I had pictured a roof over the platform and the idea hit me to build a treehouse.'

After caching his supplies in a hammock between two of the trees, Schmidt sped to Anchorage to stake his claim to the land. 'I was the fourth from the last to get a homestead, the programme shut down soon afterwards,' he says. When he returned, the following

TOP LEFT The Wilderness Treehouse Lodge evolved from an animal-proof elevated platform. It is one of the most isolated treehouses in the world. **LEFT AND ABOVE** Overlooking the Alaskan range, the treehouse is 90 miles from the nearest road. **PREVIOUS PAGE** Treehouse Hotel at the Green Iguana Sanctuary, Costa Rica (see pages 74–78).

February, there was bad news. 'The fishing lodge that I'd worked for had gone bankrupt. So much for my free flights to bring in building materials.' Instead he struck a deal to buy an archaic snowmobile, and some of their scrap pile of materials – plywood, roofing metal, windows, glass, some pipes, and an old Volkswagen bonnet. Innovating a sledge from the bonnet, Schmidt loaded the scrap and set out to build his treehouse.

'There was no preliminary design. I just used the natural spacing of the trees, and took special care not to harm the living tree,' says Schmidt. This explains the structure's asymmetrical shape. The walls are 4.75, 3.6, 3.3 and 3 metres long. Schmidt also knew that bears do not climb higher than 4.5 metres so that decided the height. The form of the treehouse was also dictated by his tools and materials, and by the time constraints imposed by the amount of food available – about two weeks.

Given the conditions it comes as little surprise that there were some problems. 'I forgot to take a spirit level, so the floor is not exactly flat. And I dropped my tape measure somewhere in nine feet of snow, so I had to improvise with a piece of rope for measurements,' says Schmidt. But the most significant problem came when the snowmobile fell on the chainsaw, bending the bar. At the time he had only finished the floor and the wall and roof supports. 'I could still cut trees, but could not make straight cuts necessary to make boards. I was determined not to give up, but what could I do?' There was just one more week before the ski plane was due to pick him up. The answer was to patch together walls from plywood and metal roofing material. 'The un-weathered wood looks horribly out of place up in the trees, but it has proved to be weatherproof and sturdy', says Schmidt.

The surprisingly spacious end product includes a small table, a queen-sized bed on an elevated platform, a woodstove for heat, a padded bench and homemade chair, a cooking area with a small stove, and windows of various sizes all around. Schmidt made the roof flat to take advantage of the mountain views. 'It's also a great place to sleep on a warm summer night, mosquitoes don't come up this high,' he says. The plan has always been to replace the plywood, but the work would require radical surgery and it has weathered a grey colour, making it look less out of place. It has also withstood strong earthquakes and tree breaking winds for over a decade.

For anybody adventurous enough, the treehouse has also become an unlikely holiday destination. Visitors have come from as far as Liechtenstein, France, Switzerland, Austria and Germany, as well as Colorado and Oregon. Schmidt's mother has even been to stay. Getting there would be sufficiently adventurous for most. During summer guests fly to a nearby lake and then hike for an hour and a half. 'I doubt most people would find it without me,' says Schmidt. To get out a further hike is required, followed by a four-mile raft downstream to another lake. During winter access is by snowmachine, a 100-mile trek.

Schmidt's treehouse does not quite cover its costs. Due to isolation and short summer seasons, guided visits are rare. But there are plans to build a new 'deluxe', sister treehouse. 'This will include a shower, flush toilet, and could sleep up to four', explains Schmidt. 'I mostly plan to have it as a two-person set up, and offer it with gourmet meals.' Schmidt is a dab hand in the kitchen. There is also the possibility of renting it in winter to ski and snowmobile enthusiasts.

TOP LEFT
During summer
months visitors fly
to a nearby lake and
then hike for an hour
and a half.

CENTRE
The Alaskan range.

TOP RIGHT
Wilderness Treehouse
Lodge is 90 miles
from the nearest road.

BELOW
The treehouse is
surprisingly spacious.
It includes a bed,
dining table and
cooking equipment.

GREEN IGUANA SANCTUARY

TREEHOUSE HOTEL PUNTA UVA, COSTA RICA

This treehouse owes its existence to the green iguana. Since 1994 Edsart Besier, a Dutch amateur botanist, has worked to preserve this critically endangered species. His Iguanaverde Foundation runs a captive breeding programme and research station within Costa Rica's Gandoca-Manzanillo Wildlife Refuge. The treehouse has become a crucial means of generating revenue for the self-funded organization.

The origins of the circular structure, whose base is 1.8 metres from the ground, go back to 1999. It began life as Besier's bathroom – a shower and toilet were shielded from the forest by a wicker screen. Since then it has evolved into a two-bedroom retreat hotel.

When Besier arrived in Costa Rica he lived in a self-built house deep inside the Gandoca-Manzanillo jungle. 'After a while I started to rent it out, to raise some money,' he says. As the rental market boomed, Besier moved into a 1950s American school bus. 'It works well, and still functions as a vehicle,' he says. But despite an inventive conversion there was no room for a bathroom. Besier muddled by for a few months until the trunk of a nearby sangrillo, a hardwood that thrives in Caribbean coastal conditions, revealed itself as a discreet solution.

Besier inserted a bathroom in the tree's natural curves and cavities. As time passed he built a wooden platform above the shower unit, as a weather shield. With the raised platform a physical reality, bedrooms and balconies were a natural progression. 'What began as a necessity, my own simple shower, has slowly evolved into this fancy treehouse,' says Besier.

He received assistance from Eduvige Alvaro Vanegas, a Nicaraguan carpenter, but the treehouse was never actually 'designed'. 'Its shape and form were dictated by the position of the trees,' explains Besier. 'They showed me what would work.' A sentiment shared by treehouse builders around the world.

In a little over a year the temporary bathroom metamorphosed into what we see today, a two-level timber dwelling connected to a ground level shack by a fixed staircase. No trees were cut down or trimmed to make way for the treehouse. The entire structure is composed of wood from fallen trees. The treehouse can accommodate five people in two rooms. The upstairs double has a private bathroom, but all guests benefit from the now extended sangrillo shower system.

It is located on Punta Uva beach, within the Iguanaverde Foundation's ocean front property, on Costa Rica's eastern seaboard. The Wildlife Refuge is home to an incredible array of wildlife, from humming birds to poison dart frogs.

The Iguanaverde Foundation was established in 2001. The not-for-profit organization is supported by private donations and whatever Besier can make. Its ambition is to nurture the population of green iguanas in the Gandoca-Manzanillo Wildlife Refuge from an unsustainable 2000 to a healthy 8000. 'We are running a programme of raising iguanas in captivity and releasing them aged one. We also talk at local schools, to raise awareness of the iguana,' says Besier.

The treehouse hotel has been open for business since March 2002. It took a while for word to get out, but Besier's website helped break the deadlock. He estimates that 80 per cent of bookings come via the internet. 'Now the treehouse is pretty much full all the time,' he says. He estimates that it makes around US$1,000–1,500 per month. 'More than enough to live on.' The only downside is that he has had to build himself a new bathroom.

LEFT Edsart Besier ascends the fixed wooden starcase to the two bedroom treehouse.

FROM LEFT
The treehouse is connected to a communal ground level shack; The shape and form of the treehouse was dictated by the position of the trees; The original shower and bathroom.

OVER PAGE
The entire structure is composed of wood from fallen trees.

A PILGRIM SITE

CHÊNE MILLÉNAIRE D'ALLOUVILLE NORMANDY, FRANCE

ABOVE The Chêne Millénaire as it looked in the early twentieth century.

RIGHT A staircase wrapped round the trunk offers access to the upper chapel.

When the common oak of Allouville first took root Vikings were still terrorizing the northern seas and the Mediterranean was under the yoke of Byzantium. Nearly thirteen centuries later it is 80 per cent hollow and accommodates two chapels. Propped up by an intricate web of cables, piles and internal scaffolding, the ancient oak makes a freakish sight.

Over the years the Chêne Millénaire has become a symbol of local identity and evidence of regional fertility. It has defied the passage of time thanks to the will of its human neighbours. To the one thousand residents of Allouville the tree is both icon and spiritual heart, a small-scale equivalent of the Sagrada Familia's hold over Barcelona.

Allouville-Bellefosse is thirty miles north-west of Rouen in the heart of Normandy. When approached from the nearby town of Yvetot, the first indication of settlement is the gleaming bulk of an aggregates factory interrupting the flat, intensely cultivated landscape. Allouville itself is set back just over a mile from the N29. With the exception of the Chêne Millénaire the village is anonymous. Nineteenth-century farm buildings blend seamlessly with contemporary homes. A café bar and scattering of owner-occupied shops exist in an atmosphere of small-scale calm.

The treehouse is located in the grounds of Saint-Quentin, the sixteenth-century village church. It is eighteen metres high and has a ground level circumference of fifteen metres, the girth betraying its prodigious age. A wood panelled lower chapel, dedicated to Notre Dame de la Paix, accommodates a miniature altar and a standing congregation of three. The second chapel, known as the 'Hermit's Chamber', is accessed via a spiral staircase attached to the outside of the tree. Internally the arrangement is almost identical. Although look up and you will see a tangle of metal supports going up the spire. A small metal cross sits on the summit.

Until the late seventeenth century the huge oak led a comparatively normal life. It was an established landmark, but nothing more. That changed in 1696 when it became a chapel. The

AVIS IL EST DEFENDU SOUS PEINE D'AMEN
D'ESCALADER LA BALUSTRADE QUI ENTO
CHÊNE, D'ENLEVER L'ECORCE ET LES RAM
DU CHÊNE, D'EN ENLEVER LES FEUILLES
PROCES VERBAL SERA DRESSE POUR
CONTREVENANTS

A NOTRE DAME DE LA PAIX
ERIGEE PAR M. L'ABBE
DU DETROIT CURE
D'ALLOUVILLE en 1696

LEFT AND ABOVE
New timber shingling
was added during the
most recent overhaul.

village pastor, Father Du Cerceau, was a long-time admirer of the gnarled giant, already a venerable 900 years old. One day, in a bid to gauge its dimensions, the priest commandeered some school children to climb inside its natural cavities. Squeezing as many children as possible into the tree would allow him to estimate its volume. The final figure was forty.

The eccentric experiment planted an idea in Father Du Cerceau's head. If the tree could accommodate so many humans, why not transform it into an extension of the church? By the end of the year a bed, chair and table had been installed in the upper chamber, and the tree had been dedicated. It functioned as a hermitage.

During the eighteenth century it was visited by two kings (Louis XV and Charles II of England). And despite a plot to raze it as a symbol of the old order, it survived the French Revolution. The villagers campaigned for clemency. But by the mid-nineteenth century weariness and weather damage meant the retreat had become uninhabitable even for humble hermits. It was time for an overhaul.

The tree took on its current appearance in 1853. After being informed of its deteriorating condition, the prefect of the Seine-Inférieure, M. Le Baron Leroy, ordered a comprehensive renovation. He wanted it to project a level of dignity appropriate to a religious monument. Under the eye of the Ecclesiastical Institute of Yvetot the two chapels were lined with fresh panels and dressed in subdued Gothic finery. A new spiral staircase was wrapped around the tree, and the upper chamber's status as a hermitage was rescinded for that was now thought too demeaning.

Perhaps the most glorious day in the tree's epic history was 3 October 1854, when the Chêne Millénaire was officially inaugurated as a seat of worship. The Archbishop of Rouen, Blanquart de Bailleul, took the inaugural mass. A poem composed for the occasion contained the lines: 'A pretty sanctuary; So much revered; Dressed by Marie; In the secular tree.' Today the Chêne hosts two masses a year on 2 July and the day after the first communion.

The intervening years have brought storms – there was a particularly bad one in 1912, after which some branches had to be reinforced – and persistent rumours of demise. The tree's most recent surgery was carried out in 1988–89. After prolonged debate it was decided to spend two million francs out of regional funds to prop it up in perpetuity. For the first time the tree became more artifice than natural phenomenon.

Only the younger north-facing side still comes into leaf. It is the tree's ghost that inhabits the graveyard.

ABOVE TOP
The two chapels are lined with timber panels and dressed in subdued Gothic finery.

ABOVE
Ropes, harnesses and scaffolding support the ancient tree.

RIGHT
The tree is now more artifice than natural phenomenon.

AMBITIOUS DREAMS

BIG BEACH IN THE SKY HAINAN, CHINA

ABOVE The three-storey
treehouse sits in
a tamarind tree.

Big Beach in the Sky is the largest of four treehouses at a holiday resort on the Chinese island of Hainan. The impressive three-storey structure sits in a mighty tamarind tree overlooking the beach near the city of Sanya. It was devised by David Greenberg, an entrepreneur based in Hawaii. The name reflects a magic mushroom induced moment of supreme contentment in 1972.

Although a trained architect, Greenberg has clear views on the value of formal design. 'I am an anti-architect, which might be described as working with nature as opposed to building little boxes for people. Treehouses are very anti-architecture. I did once try to design a treehouse [Greenberg has also built a treehouse resort on his home island of Maui, Hawaii]. But nothing came out.'

The Hainan resort was developed by Greenberg's company, Treehouses of Hawaii, in association with a local Chinese tourist agency. The Sino-US joint venture was facilitated by a deal between the administrations of both provinces – Hainan and Hawaii are twinned.

To build the structures Greenberg recruited Michael Garnier, an experienced treehouse designer based in Oregon in the United States. Work began in early 1999. 'I took Garnier over to act as engineer. He helped me with one or two basic forms, and some of the platforms, and then we started arguing a lot,' recalls Greenberg. One morning, about two weeks into construction, Greenberg woke up to find that Garnier had left. [Garnier has nothing positive to say about the experience.]

From that point on, with some of the treehouses partially built, Greenberg worked independently. 'On all my treehouses I like to see how the tree speaks to me. For the Big Beach in the Sky I sketched the whole thing out at full scale in bamboo, to see what would work.'

Access to the Big Beach is at the top of a six metre sand dune. A small pagoda-like treehouse leads to a ten metre long suspension bridge. The first level communal area is open to the elements on all sides. A half-height balustrade offers some safety from the ten metre drop, while offering 360 degree views. The two sleeping levels upstairs are enclosed, with a combination of bamboo walls and glass, to expose the views. There are two double bedrooms.

Staircases, furniture, and the viewing platforms were all hand-carved by local craftspeople. 'Fantastically skilled people,' recalls Greenberg. The dark-stained hardwood suggests luxury and permanence.

To date the Big Beach in the Sky has struggled to make money. 'The Chinese are big fans of treehouses, and there has been great interest since the treehouses opened, but not many visitors stay overnight. Money has been hard to come by for the local people,' laments Greenberg. It is also rather in the shadow of an 800 hectare Buddhist theme park.

Undaunted, Greenberg has expanded his outlook. He now has plans to build treehouse resorts on four beaches around the Pacific Rim (see also Tropical Treehouse Competition, pages 148–149).

ABOVE The mezzanine level: Dark-stained hardwood was used for the floorboards and fixed staircase.

HOISTED TO THE SKY

GREEN MAGIC TREEHOUSE RESORT KERALA, INDIA

The Keralan rainforest is 1200 metres above sea level. A further 27 metres up in the leafy canopy are two treehouses. The Green Magic resort is not for the faint hearted.

The nearest town with transport links is Calicut, from where a bus climbs forty miles into the mountains, passing plantations of ginger, rubber, tea and coffee en route. The road runs out at Vythiri, about half an hour from Green Magic. The final stretch is by four-wheel drive.

Green Magic is an eco-resort set in 500 acres of rainforest. As well as the two treehouses, which are set about a mile apart, there are four ground-based lodges – 'for those who like the attitude, but not the altitude', reads the brochure.

The treehouses were built over five months in 1990 by local Paniya tribesmen, many of whom were forced from their tribal lands during the 1970s when the Indian government conferred national heritage status on the rainforest. It was the Paniya's traditional erumadam tree platforms, from which herds were guarded, that provided the inspiration for the hotel. Both houses, which occupy enormous ficus trees, have two storeys, wraparound balconies, coir matting and thatched roofs. Bathrooms, complete with functioning showers and toilets, are on the upper levels.

One of the more extraordinary features is the water-powered lift. Instead of pressing a call button you turn a tap, and leave it running for ten minutes while a black bag fills with water. When the bag is full, the counter-weight hoists visitors to the sky in a cane lift. For the other treehouse there is a steep climb and a hanging rope bridge to negotiate before reaching the safety of the treehouse.

Green Magic is an ecologically sensitive holiday destination. All food, power and water are locally sourced – bullock dung powers the cookers and water is diverted from mountain streams. Forest trekking is among the more popular back-to-nature events to occupy guests. But such is the sense of place at Green Magic, that what visitors actually do becomes a secondary concern. Most are happy to pass the time up in their trees – sunsets are particularly spectacular. In fact there is very little need to descend. Food and drink are sent up by a pulley system. All guests have to do is call 'cuckoo'.

LEFT FROM TOP A rope bridge offers access to one of the two treehouses; Bed with mosquito net; Beds are open to the elements. **RIGHT** A water-powered lift transports guests to their rooms.

LEFT AND RIGHT Both treehouses have two storeys. The Green Magic eco-resort occupies over 500 acres of rainforest.

LEFT AND RIGHT
Beacons in the
Indian night – views
are particularly
spectacular at
sunset.

WOODPECKER HOTEL

HOTELL HACKSPETT VÄSTERÅS, SWEDEN

Hotell Hackspett (Woodpecker Hotel) began life as an installation. Mikael Genberg wanted to show his paintings and sculptures in a less formal environment than galleries and museums. 'The treehouse was a means of "capturing" people in a more direct way. I wanted to completely surround them with my work for a couple of hours or even a night. The treehouse was the art.' At least that was the idea in 1996.

The following year, when the treehouse was complete, it was clear that Genberg could not maintain it for nothing. So he began charging. It has since accommodated over 500 guests, and is a well-established landmark in the small town of Västerås (population 130,000), 62 miles west of Stockholm.

Hotell Hackspett would not have got off the ground at all without the enlightened support of Tapio Hovebro, then head of culture and tourism for Västerås. If Genberg was going to entice enthusiasts inside, the treehouse needed to be in a prominent location. A 350-year-old oak in Vasaparken, the largest park in town was his preference. 'Tapio thought the treehouse installation was a great idea, but he also thought that it would be difficult to convince the town hall to let me do it.' Fortunately he was wrong. Permission was granted, and work began soon afterwards.

Genberg wanted to build in sympathy with nature. No nails were used to support the treehouse. Instead it is suspended from wires 13 metres up in the tree. The timber base sits in a four-branch fork, creating a firm foundation. 'It means that in strong winds the tree and cabin sway together.'

The treehouse comprises an open-plan living space, complete with a single bed, table, chair, hammock, bookshelf, kitchenette, and heater. There is also a toilet,

LEFT Woodpecker Hotel sits in a 350-year-old oak tree.

and there's a balcony from which to enjoy the sunset. For safety, it also comes equipped with fire extinguisher.

Be warned, Hotell Hackspett is not necessarily for the elderly or very young. Guests do need to haul themselves up on a rudimentary access rope, although in exceptional circumstances Genberg does have a block and tackle system, a 'type of elevator', that has hauled guests as old as eighty-seven into the old oak. Once ensconced, there is no need to come down. The hotel is half-board. Meals are hoisted up in a basket.

The small cabin (the base measures 2.5m x 3m) was almost entirely self-built. Only when it was nearing completion were friends recruited to help add the finishing touches, including the paintwork – red with white gables, in keeping with local tradition.

Since completing the Hotell Hackspett Genberg has also built Utter-Inn, an underwater hotel on Lake Malaren, near Västerås. It comprises a waterproof tank suspended three metres under water from a fixed platform. He is now working with the Swedish Space Company on Luna Resort, a plan to build a house on the moon. 'Of course that too will be red with white gables.'

Hotell Hackspett is open from May to October.

FAR LEFT The red and white paintwork is in keeping with local tradition.

LEFT Meals are hoisted up in baskets.

OPEN TO THE SKIES

WEST BAY TREEHOUSE ROATAN, HONDURAS

As a young man in the 1970s Foster Diaz wanted a quiet place for contemplation, and romancing. So he created the West Bay treehouse, high in the branches of a century old mango tree overlooking the Caribbean Sea on the island of Roatan. The simple wooden structure is surrounded by white, powdery beaches and dense mangrove. Tropical undergrowth and flowering trees roll gently up to the hills behind.

In its short life the treehouse has been pulled apart by a violent hurricane and rebuilt as part of a small colony of rental villas. It began life as a fairly rudimentary wooden platform, without sides or a roof. The objective of privacy was achieved through its height and the thick mango foliage that made it all but invisible from the ground during the summer months.

Over the years Foster improved the structure, adding walls, a roof, and fashioning a self-supporting spiral staircase. Impressively, all the work was carried out by hand. With no electricity supply, Foster and his brothers did not have the luxury of power tools or machine production techniques.

During the 1980s Foster and his family began to build a number of beachfront cabanas as holiday rentals for adventurous tourists – Roatan is 42 miles north of Honduras. In response to an increasing number of enquiries, Foster began to let out the treehouse for short stays. This was how things continued until 27 October 1998 when Hurricane Mitch, the fourth strongest hurricane ever recorded in the Atlantic Basin, seriously damaged the treehouse.

Much of the spiral staircase survived the battering, but the remains of the original base were unsalvageable. In the years since Foster has built a new treehouse. The principal difference is that the walls are only waist high, allowing 360 degree views and being less vulnerable to strong winds. With the house open to the elements, visitors fall asleep to the sound of rustling leaves and rolling ocean.

Other differences include a toilet, running water and an electricity supply, which was also useful in the construction process. A balcony large enough to accommodate a hammock is in the front.

ABOVE TOP West Bay treehouse sits in a century-old mango tree.

ABOVE Access is via a timber spiral staircase.

RIGHT The treehouse overlooks the Caribbean. It was substantially rebuilt following a hurricane in 1998.

Roatan is a long, thin island, surrounded by the world's second largest barrier reef. For centuries the reef was an extremely effective defence against water-based armies and so Roatan was an ideal hide-out for pirates. Among the residents was the British buccaneer Sir Henry Morgan, regarded as one of the most successful, decorated and debauched privateers ever to roam the Indies. During the 1660s and 1670s he used Roatan as a base from which to ravage and plunder the Spanish-held Central American mainland. According to local legend the loot from Morgan's 1671 raid on Panama is buried somewhere on Roatan.

An earlier visitor was Christopher Columbus, who is said to have discovered the island on his fourth and final voyage in 1512. He was particularly taken with the drinking water, having not previously tasted 'sweeter water of better quality'. Later, as a British protectorate, Roatan became a dumping ground for rebellious slaves. Their descendants still live on the island. Although the island has been governed by Honduras since 1860, most residents still speak English.

Free blacks from the Cayman Islands also made their home on Roatan. Diaz's great grandfather was a Cayman Islander. When he arrived on Roatan he settled on a beachfront site, the same site that today houses Diaz's rental resort and treehouse.

LEFT AND RIGHT Walls are waist-high, allowing 360 degree views and reducing the 'sail effect'.

ROOMS WITH A VIEW

CEDAR CREEK TREEHOUSE NEAR ASHFORD, WASHINGTON, USA

ABOVE The enclosed observation deck.

RIGHT Cedar Creek treehouse optimizes views over the Sawtooth Ridge and Mount Rainier.

The Cedar Creek treehouse must be among the most homely anywhere in the world. Despite hovering 15 metres above ground level this double-deck treehouse is equipped with sleeping space for five, a sunroom, fully-operational kitchen, and an impressive fixed staircase. It has also been built to make the most of the stunning scenery, with views of the Sawtooth Ridge and Mount Rainier, as well as the abundant wildlife and meteor showers. It must be one of the only treehouses to have featured in the pages of *Fine Homebuilding* magazine.

The Cedar Creek treehouse began life in the summer of 1981, soon after Bill Compher and his wife – both professional folk musicians – had bought a heavily forested plot of land on the edge of Gifford Pinchot National Forest, about six and a half miles south-east of Ashford. 'I built the treehouse in the summers of 1981 and 1982. I lived there on and off for two years while we built our home on the ground,' explains Compher, a man with a passion for heights.

The original access was a basic wooden ladder, which allowed Compher to clear branches to make space for the treehouse. He used ropes and pulleys to haul up tools, nails and wood to build the platform, which is bolted to the tree and stabilized by guy wires. Then he added walls, windows, a roof, a front door and furnishings. The treehouse is wrapped around the trunk of a 200-year-old red cedar. It has a five square metre base, which accommodates a living room, kitchen, bathroom and sunroom. The second storey has sleeping space for four. Food is kept cool in an icebox and cooked on a butane stove. Solar panels power 12-volt electric lights.

In the early 1990s Compher decided to turn the treehouse into a holiday rental. The key difference was the construction of a new stairwell, although confirmation that it was required had come a little earlier when Compher's mother-in-law froze ten metres up the ladder.

The reassuringly solid replacement was built between 1993 and 1997. It is constructed of recycled wood, tied together by 30 centimetre long bolts, and ascends to around 13 metres in ten increments. At the top Compher has built a short enclosed bridge to the treehouse.

Shortly after opening the treehouse as a rental destination Compher began work on a new one, which he planned as an observation deck around the trunk of an epic Douglas fir 12 metres away. The octagonal crow's nest, with a domed roof made of aluminium retrieved from Boeing Surplus, is 25 metres above ground. Originally access was via a wooden ladder attached to the side of the tree – visitors had to strap on climbing harnesses, clip themselves to a safety rope,

and then climb. Fortunately that tricky ascent is no longer necessary. In 2001 Compher's son, Cedar, designed and built a spiral staircase around the tree, making things a lot easier. The climb is worth the effort. The observatory is equipped with a telescope and binoculars for star-gazing.

During Easter 2004 the observatory and treehouse were linked together by 'Rainbow Bridge', so named because of the kaleidoscope of colours on the top and underside. The 15 metre rope bridge was built on terra firma and hoisted into place 25 metres above ground.

Over the past two decades Compher's creation has generated a great deal of attention, most of it good. But back in the 1980s it was a magnet for helicopter pilots training at nearby Fort Lewis. On and off for years the family's solitude was shattered by hovering helicopters. They protested to the army and to their congressman, but the flights continued. Then Compher called his congressman, demanded a face-to-face meeting and added that he planned to invite every newspaper and radio and TV station in the area to send a reporter. The flights ceased the next day.

Cedar Creek is open for visits throughout the year, but the weather is unpredictable so the wise keep in touch with Compher before travelling.

LEFT Rainbow Bridge links the treehouse to the observatory.

BELOW A fixed staircase offers access to the two-deck treehouse.

TREETOP MEETINGS

ACKERGILL TOWER BY WICK, CAITHNESS, SCOTLAND

Ackergill Tower is a fifteenth-century estate at the very tip of Scotland, just down the road from John O'Groats. It is perched on the top of a cliff overlooking the wild seascapes of Caithness, one of Britain's less celebrated natural wonders.

The estate is a luxury retreat for the super wealthy. It is among the world's more exclusive destinations for corporate meetings. Facilities include an opera house, twenty-five luxury bedrooms, clay pigeon and rifle shooting, a private fishing loch, and a billiard room. During the summer months, when Ackergill is bathed in the midnight sun thanks to its northerly location, visitors can spend the evening over a leisurely round of golf, after a day spent stag hunting in the Highlands. It also boasts a treehouse conference centre, the only one of its kind in Europe.

Ackergill's treehouse was designed by John Harris of the TreeHouse Company, which is based in Fenwick at the other end of Scotland. At the time of its completion in spring 2003 it was the largest in Britain; now it has been superseded by the Alnwick Castle treehouse (see pages 108–113).

The luxurious circular treehouse is located inside a large walled garden. It is supported 3.5 metres above the ground in six 150-year-old sycamore trees. Although the base is partially supported by posts sunk in the ground, John Harris believes that the structure still deserves to be seen as a treehouse as opposed to a house around a tree. 'Branches extend throughout the five-metre high volume, it's completely entwined in the woodland,' explains the designer. The main door, at the top of the fixed spiral staircase, is reached by stepping between two large tree trunks. A third trunk runs through the reception area and out of the roof.

At a total cost of around £200,000, the Ackergill treehouse is finished to a very high specification. The conference centre has a floor area of 65 square metres. In its boardroom format it has a capacity of thirty. When used as a theatre it has space for a forty-strong audience. It also includes a fully-equipped professional kitchen.

The location and history of the trees has contributed to their unusual strength and size. Over the years the self-seeded sycamores have grown fit and strong in the shelter of the fertile Victorian garden, which has 5.5 metre high walls. But they are quite stunted. Every time the trees have popped their heads above the walls they have been exposed to the full force of the Scottish weather and pulled their heads back in. A further benefit of the wall is that it dramatically reduces the 'sail effect', which has significance for the prolonged well-being of both the sycamores and the treehouse.

TOP LEFT The treehouse is supported by six 150-year-old sycamore trees.

BOTTOM RIGHT Posts sunk in the ground provide additional support.

BOTTOM LEFT A verandah surrounds the treehouse.

ABOVE The treehouse is entwined in the woodland.

A TREEHOUSE FOR EVERYONE

TREEHOUSE AT THE ALNWICK GARDEN NORTHUMBERLAND, ENGLAND

BELOW The small village
of treehouses occupies
an entire copse.

The treehouse at The Alnwick Garden is among the largest, most expensive, and lavishly-equipped ever built. To describe it in the singular is misleading. It is really a small village of treehouses linked by a web of suspended walkways. Its setting is equally impressive, overlooking a Northumberland landscape designed by Capability Brown, one of Britain's most revered eighteenth-century landscape designers.

The £3.3 million treehouse, which opened to the public at the beginning of 2005, occupies a copse of mature lime and beech trees a short walk from Alnwick Castle, the ancient seat of the Duke of Northumberland. Younger readers might recognize the castle from the Harry Potter films, in which it doubled as Hogwarts School of Witchcraft and Wizardry.

The idea came from a visit to France. 'I saw a treehouse at Euro Disney and I thought, "everyone loves treehouses",' explains the Duchess of Northumberland, who ironically is not a great one for heights.

The 17-metre-high complex includes an 80-seat restaurant, a shop, and acres of timber-decked satellite walkways hanging in the trees. Other features include the Roost, a room suspended separately from the main treehouse, which sways gently in the wind. This is one of the two main education rooms, designed to host The Alnwick Garden's learning programmes. The other is the Nest, a turret right at the top of the main structure. Throughout the year gardening, painting and cooking courses keep children occupied, while their parents wander in the gardens below.

The treehouse also incorporates elevated walkways made of rope. 'It is designed to be "safely dangerous". I want the treehouse and the garden to be hands-on experiences, not too manicured or formal', says the Duchess.

'Many children now have less opportunity to play than any other generation. The idea is to provide a challenge, and include elements of risk, so that you can help children better equip themselves for the future. And why shouldn't the less able-bodied, of all ages, go high up and see life from the trees?' she adds. The walkways are wide enough to accommodate wheelchairs and buggies. Looking to the future, the Duchess has plans for the addition of a further adventure playground under the walkways.

Because it is so big – the treehouse covers an area the size of two Olympic swimming pools – total direct support by the copse of sixteen mature trees was impossible. Strength and stability are ensured by two concrete towers underneath the main buildings. Timber braces provide further support.

The entrance to the main body of the treehouse is via a curving ramp, which allows wheelchair access. There is enough space for 300 visitors at any one time.

The treehouse has been designed to project a sense of organic evolution. Oak bark covers the towers. The buildings are asymmetrical and clad in recycled wood, rough sawn boarding, and 'distressed' timber. Windows of different shapes, sizes and colours

LEFT The treehouse and walkways are accessible by wheelchair.

BELOW AND RIGHT Recycled wood, rough sawn boarding, distressed timber and asymmetrical windows project a sense of organic evolution.

OVER PAGE The 17-metre-high complex includes a restaurant, shop and acres of walkways.

have been placed randomly to enhance the quirky appearance. It is stage-managed but idiosyncratic.

Contemporary materials and preservation techniques have been employed to ensure safety and longevity. Windows are made of 6mm polycarbonate to provide protection from stray branches, and the timber has been pre-treated with a pressure injection system to avoid rot and decay. The treehouse uses materials from sustainable sources and includes Canadian cedar, Siberian larch, Scandinavian redwood and English and Scots pine.

The final scheme is the product of several designers and treehouse consultants. In 2001 an original design was dreamed up by John Harris, an experienced treehouse designer based in Fenwick, a short distance over the border in Scotland. Following some revisions the project was taken up by a local architectural practice Napper Architects.

The interior of the treehouse has been enhanced by Paul Doran, a film set designer. The Duchess also recruited Brummie Stokes, a former member of the SAS, to advise on the design of the elevated walkways, particularly the provision of disabled access. Since 1991 Stokes and his wife Lynn have run the Taste for Adventure Centre, a registered charity and outdoor centre for less privileged children. Stokes is working with Richter Spielgerate GmbH, a German manufacturer of playground equipment, to design and build the aerial playground.

Since the mid-1990s the Duchess has been nurturing The Alnwick Garden, a new walled visitor attraction, managed by The Alnwick Garden Trust, an independent registered charity. Through the ages, the five-hectare site has been the focus of fevered horticultural activity – there is evidence of at least six former gardens under the site. Today it has been revived as one of Britain's most popular horticultural attractions. The garden itself was designed by Belgian landscape architect Jacques Wirtz and his son Peter. Its centrepiece is the Grand Cascade, an epic water feature. The treehouse forms part of the second phase of development, which also includes a poison garden, and a new pavilion and visitor centre.

PRIVATE TREEHOUSES

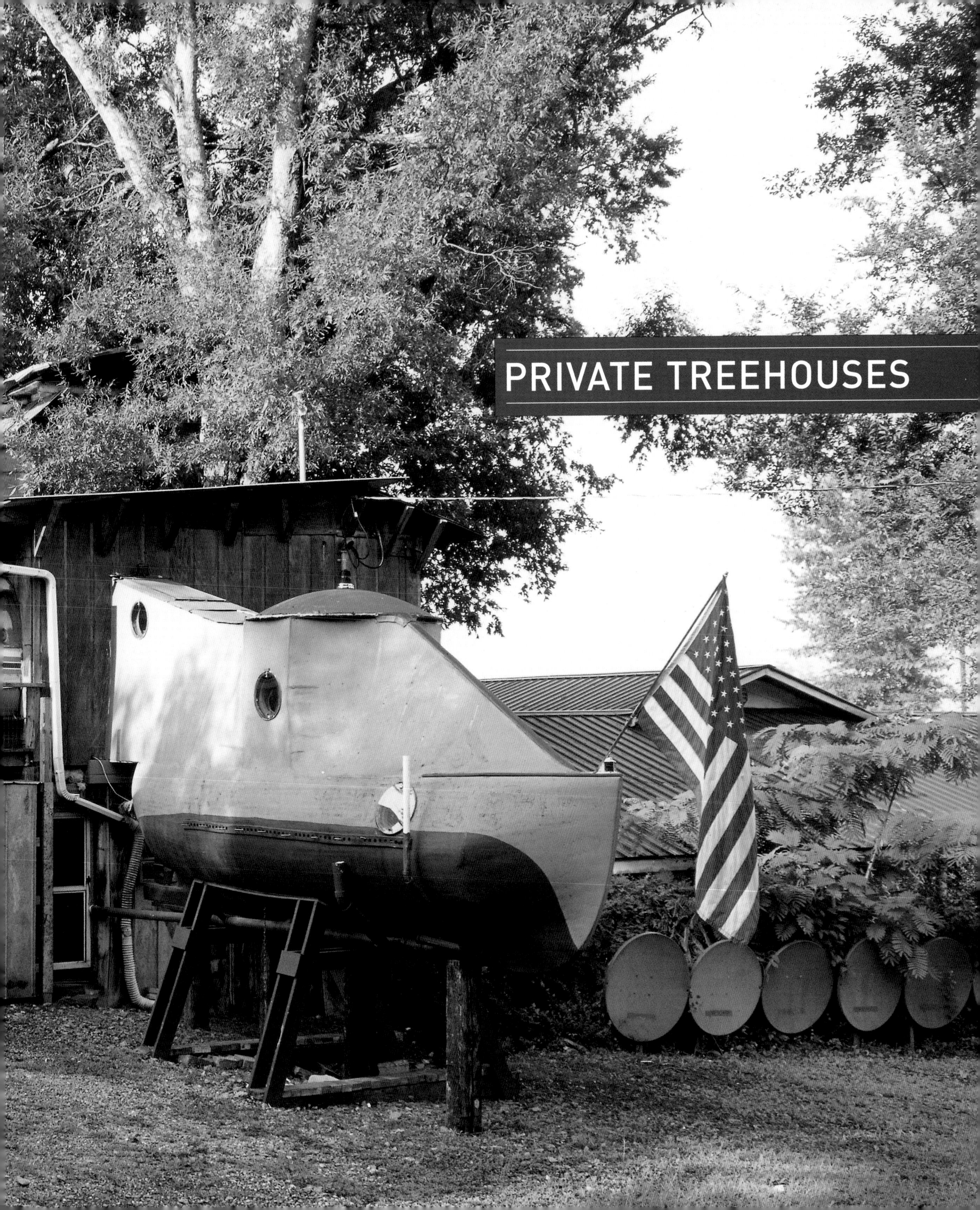

HUMAN NEST

JOHN MALKOVICH'S TREEHOUSE PROVENCE, FRANCE

This willow nest-like treehouse, designed for actor John Malkovich, was the culmination of an installation by British land sculptor Clare Wilks.

Malkovich's Provence home overlooks the Lubéron Valley, due east of Avignon. On the horizon sits a romantic ruined castle – once believed to be home to the Marquis de Sade. The landscape is hot, dry and windblown. In 1995 until its disintegration some years later, the human nest was embedded within it.

The connection between client and designer dates back to the summer of 1993 when Malkovich was appearing in Covent Garden. He and his young son became regulars at the Phoenix Garden, a small public space near the theatre. The following year a residents' group was lobbying for a treehouse to be built in the garden and Malkovich contributed some funds. The designer, Clare Wilks, proposed a fantastical composition of three teardrop-shaped wooden cocoons sitting in trees. Unfortunately the residents found it impossible to secure planning permission to build a treehouse in a public place. The idea came to nothing. And that would have been the end of the story had Malkovich not been intrigued by Wilks's proposal.

'He phoned me out of the blue and asked if we could meet,' says Wilks. That summer Wilks was resident artist at Hillier's Arboretum in Hampshire. One weekend Malkovich and his family made the trip down from London. Across one of the lawns at the arboretum Wilks had designed a series of her trademark willow nests. Children were climbing all over them.

'I like the idea of people being able to get inside my work,' says Wilks. Malkovich was impressed, and asked Wilks to propose some play structures for his new home in Provence.

His garden is about the size of two football pitches. Along one side is a line of mature hazel stools, shielding a vineyard. An old walnut tree marks the corner of the property. Wilks proposed that a

TOP A willow tunnel led to the nest.
LEFT Access was via a fixed ladder.

RIGHT The nest could accommodate two adults.

PREVIOUS PAGE Sam Edwards's treehouse (see pages 122–127).

ABOVE The willow tunnel viewed from the nest.

willow nest be woven into the walnut tree, tying it to the landscape. This would be linked by a bridge to a second treehouse supported in the adjacent hazel stool. A fixed ladder would provide access.

Malkovich made some revisions to the initial sketch. He would have liked a second bridge to stretch to the next tree. And he wondered whether the entrance could be through the willow nest, rather than at the other end. 'Malkovich had much more input than most clients. He was very design conscious,' says Wilks.

The final design was dictated as much by nature as by personal preference. Wilks was determined that the composition be embedded in the landscape. As far as possible, all materials were renewable and locally sourced.

Work began in the late spring of 1995. Wilks travelled to Provence with carpenter Henry Russell, a specialist in green wood, who assisted and offered structural advice. To create a robust frame for the tree nest, mulberry and hazel poles were fixed in a circular arrangement around the top of the walnut's trunk. For the next eleven days the hardwood poles, integrated with the branches, were woven with willow, creating the impression of a wasp's nest. Holes were left for the door and windows and Russell fashioned a flat floor from found boards. The tree nest's base was 3.5 metres from the ground. It could accommodate two adults, one standing up.

In place of the second treehouse originally proposed, a willow tunnel was built. A short bridge between the tree nest and tunnel was improvised using two poles, from which a platform of logs was suspended. A fixed ladder, rising around three metres was made from an old pole. 'Malkovich wanted something to give the children an element of risk,' explains Wilks.

That tunnel and the nest were the elevated features of the composition, but they did not mark the end of it. At the bottom of the ladder another willow tunnel led into a small arbour. The next stop was a woven wicker tower six metres high, sitting within a hazel stool. A spiral staircase ascended to a hammock slung about halfway up, with a view to the top of the tower. Earth-filled seats, a raised walkway, and a pumpkin bed – as requested by Malkovich's wife – completed the arrangement, which stretched the length of the garden, a distance of about 30 metres. But there can be no doubt the willow nest was the crowning glory.

Willow disintegrates rapidly. Within a few years the nest melted back into the landscape. But there is nothing to stop the frame being rewoven with a new structure. The children might have outgrown it, but they were not the only people to use it. 'Malkovich often took friends up there,' says Wilks.

ABOVE A ground-based tunnel of rooted willow led to the triumvirate of ladder, elevated tunnel, and nest.

CZECH FREEDOM

PROKOP ZAVADA'S PRIVATE RETREAT CHOLIN, CZECH REPUBLIC

The protest treehouses built at Fairmile in 1995 (see page 62) were the inspiration for Prokop Zavada's weekend retreat. While on holiday in the UK, Zavada and his brother spent ten days with the anti-road campaigners. 'I was sympathetic to the protestors' cause, but for me the most inspiring feature of the camp was the treehouses. Some were 15–20 metres above the ground,' says Zavada. 'They were quite small. From the ground they looked like nests.' He was hooked.

Back in the Czech Republic Zavada and friends set about building their own treehouse. 'It wasn't motivated by a violation of our rights. We just wanted somewhere peaceful. A place to escape to, and talk with friends,' Zavada explains.

They chose Male Kolo (Small Circle), a tenth-century circular fort next to the bank of the river Vltava. The fort, about an hour's drive north of Prague, has long since been reclaimed by forest. A series of Soviet-era excavations around Male Kolo had revealed pottery splinters and medieval stone brickwork. But of greatest interest to Zavada was the discovery of an embankment of wooden foundations at the highest point of the man-made mound. 'We'd like to believe that they are the remains of an ancient observation post, from where the Celts and Slovans scanned the horizon for enemies,' says Zavada.

What is certain is that the site's isolation and excellent defences mean that a modern-day treehouse can be built there without fear of intrusion. 'We didn't ask for permission, and until 2004 we never had any problems,' says Zavada. 'There was one occasion when police officers interrogated us, suspecting we were illegal Ukrainian immigrants. When they realized we were harmless, they asked why we didn't have a barrel of beer and some girls up there.' (The Czech authorities asked Zavada to remove the treehouses in 2004.)

Zavada, his friends and family built two treehouses at Male Kolo. Their appearance betrayed their inspiration. The first had a square platform; the second was triangular. Both were composed of pine, spruce and oak logs. They occupied two young oaks about six metres apart, and sit ten metres up in the branches. The treehouses were linked by a cargo net, creating a giant mid-air hammock, which was terrifying. 'I really liked the nets at Fairmile,' says Zavada.

The trees each had three trunks with diameters of 30 centimetres. This meant that both platforms were connected to at least two slim trunks. Oak logs were lifted with pulleys to make the base. Zavada used as few nails as possible. To create the foundation, logs were balanced in crotches and shuffled around until level. They were then secured with ropes. The installation of floorboards two years later improved comfort levels significantly.

Half-height walls were built around the sides of the platform, leaving space for a small balcony. Initially hazel poles were used to create a roof frame, which was covered in whatever was available – clothes, leaves, tent fabric ... 'I must confess they were really summer treehouses. There's not much shelter in winter, although I have stayed in spring and autumn,' says Zavada.

In the years since the first platform was built maintenance was minimal. In 2003 Zavada, now a geologist in his mid-twenties, replaced a foundation post and some of the hazel walls perished. A glowing testament to an (almost) nail-free treehouse. 'I'm absolutely convinced that nature provides all the materials for good tree living,' he says.

Zavada was also proudly public spirited. As well as friends and family the treehouses were used regularly by passing strangers. A guest book in a bin provided a record of visitors. Entries included numerous queries about the best way to get down and a painting of a tree-dwelling Sioux Indian. 'Above all I wanted to maintain it for all the people that liked it,' says Zavada.

TOP LEFT Both treehouses were supported by at least two oaks.

BOTTOM LEFT Panoramic views over woodland on the banks of the river Vltava.

TOP RIGHT Zavada was inspired by British protest treehouses of the mid-1990s.

BOTTOM RIGHT Access hatch. The treehouses were composed of pine, spruce and oak.

FLYING HIGH

SAM EDWARDS'S TREEHOUSE CALHOUN, GEORGIA, USA

Sam Edwards used to work as an aide to President Jimmy Carter. Today he lives in a treehouse composed largely of vehicular salvage. He and his treehouse have quite a story.

In 1990, after two decades away, Edwards returned home to Calhoun, a 'carpet town' of about 100,000 in the Appalachian foothills of North Georgia. Over sixty per cent of the world's carpets are manufactured within a fifty mile radius. After getting through more than thirty jobs in twenty years, Edwards had settled on a career as a writer. His last book was a memoir, *From Outhouse to White House to Treehouse*. The outhouse refers to a stint as a cleaner while studying at law school. 'I came home ostensibly to write another book but got tangled up with an old friend in the restaurant business,' says Edwards. 'I told him if I was going to get involved with the catering trade I was going to need somewhere to write.' Adjacent to the steak and barbecue restaurant was a small patch of woodland. His partner told him: 'Go up there and build yourself something'.

Edwards walked into the woods, found a 150-year-old 18 metre oak and envisaged a treehouse. 'I thought, if I could build a little platform up there, and run an electric cable from the restaurant, I'd have a nifty place to write.' The restaurant venture did not work out. Edwards withdrew after a year – it is now a Tex-Mex establishment which holds no interest for him. But Edwards and his three dogs still live behind it.

Since work began in 1991, Edwards has built 130 square metres of space spread over three levels and eleven rooms. Although the body of the treehouse is supported on eight wooden piles sunk around the trunk, each room incorporates a growing branch. Much of the treehouse is composed of found objects, giving it a distinctly eccentric appearance. He started out collecting windows from an abandoned train depot, corrugated iron from an old barn and pine flooring from a former slave cabin. But over the years the additions have become increasingly unconventional. Edwards has incorporated an abandoned boat, part of a prop submarine from a 1960s Elvis Presley film, and the back end of a small passenger airplane, for which he paid US$300, the only construction cost. The plane now functions as a bedroom.

What started out as a short-term necessity has become a fulltime home. The bottom tier acts as a garage and a three-room carpentry studio. The middle level incorporates a bathroom (the submarine), a kitchen,

RIGHT The original treehouse has been enclosed by vehicular salvage and ground-level shacks.

reception, dining room, office, library and guest bedroom (the boat). Edwards sleeps in the loft (6 x 3.5 metres).

The treehouse is also a work in progress. Edwards is on the look out for a 'rocket ship' to add to the mélange. He also has his eye on a ten metre high T-Rex that was a prop at a miniature golf course.

The organic evolution of the treehouse meant that planning consent was sought retrospectively. And given the restaurant's location 200 metres from Calhoun courthouse in the town centre, it took some explaining. 'I told the city inspector that I regretted putting him in a difficult position, and that I really didn't mean to build it, that it was sort of an evolution of a mistake,' says Edwards. 'The inspector shook his head, looked up and said, "I don't believe that could be put any better".'

There is no doubting its resilience. The treehouse survived a tornado in May 2002, although the tree did not fare quite so well, shedding four branches. But this was nothing compared with the carnage wreaked on the town.

Edwards was always interested in treehouses. 'My first was around the age of six. I built a three-tree triangle head high to me off the ground.' He continued to build increasingly elaborate structures, including one fifteen metres high, with five storeys, until his teens.

'Whatever happens, I intend to be buried here,' says Edwards of his treehouse. 'All my friends see this house as an extension of my eclectic but otherwise indefinable personality. Whatever that means.'

LEFT Almost every room incorporates a growing branch. **ABOVE** An old boat has become the guest bedroom.

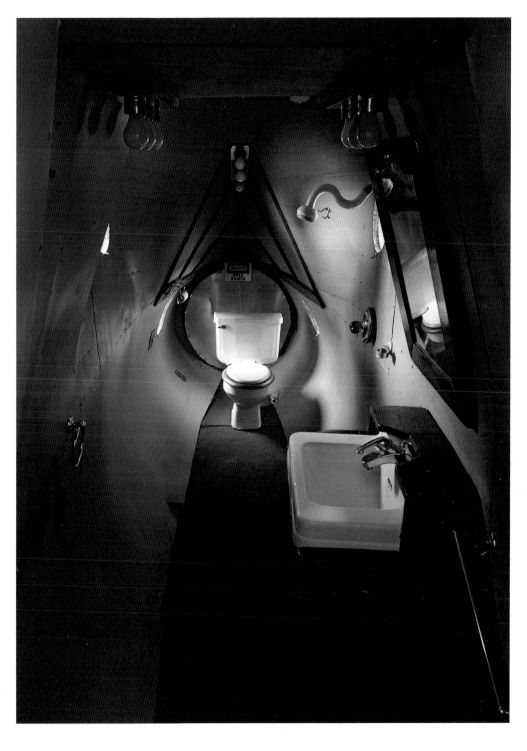

LEFT The airplane is now a bedroom.

ABOVE The prop submarine from a 1960s Elvis film is used as a bathroom.

DRINKS FOR TWO

MIRABEL OSLER'S TREESEAT SHROPSHIRE, ENGLAND

ABOVE The treeseat is perched between four alders.

RIGHT An elevated vantage point from which to enjoy the garden.

Once upon a time farmers watched over their livestock from platforms built in trees. In East Africa and India many still do. Today the rural dwellers of Middle England use tree platforms to admire their gardens and perhaps hoist up a couple of glasses and a bottle of wine.

Richard Craven, a forester and self-trained craftsman, came up with this ingenious 'treeseat' for the garden writer Mirabel Osler and her husband. They wanted to join the birds for a view over their Shropshire garden. 'Mirabel loves to sit in her wild garden. She can never understand why people spend so long tending their gardens, and so little time sitting in them. She was very proud of the roses in her orchard. But they'd never sat above the garden, and enjoyed a glass of wine. So they asked me to help,' explains Craven.

Osler had thought there would be a spiral stair but the trees were slender so Craven built a discreet platform with space for two, perched between four alders in a copse overlooking the garden. The base was about a metre deep and two metres long with the two seats opposite each other. The way up was via a delicate two-tier fixed staircase, the most complex piece of the ensemble. Everything was made of cleft oak, to blend with the woodland setting.

A stream ran conveniently nearby, so in the morning Osler would plunge in a bottle of wine. The bottle and two glasses were hoisted up after the day's work. If it happened to be windy the disconcerted pair could find themselves wondering if the swaying was real or imaginary.

The treeseat was built at the end of the 1980s and was only designed to last ten years or so, but although Osler, now widowed, has left the house, her daughter's family still enjoy it. The design is typical of Craven's work in its sympathy to both location and materials. 'Once I know a building's purpose I want to know the client and how they hope to feel when they're in it. This will indicate atmosphere. Should it be bold or secretive and mysterious, amusing or solemn, flamboyant or austere?'

Mirabel Osler's original idea was to capture 'the feeling of being in a bird's nest'.

STAR WARS FANTASY

EWOK VILLAGE OXFORDSHIRE, ENGLAND

The Ewoks, a mythical tribe of tree-dwelling teddy bears, are among the true legends of treehouses. They secured their place in human hearts thanks to an appearance in *Return of the Jedi*, the final instalment of the Star Wars films, in which they assist Luke Skywalker and his allies to destroy the energy shield that protects the Death Star. Although fictional, the Ewoks and their tree villages were based on the Korowai tribe of Irian Jaya, Indonesia (see pages 56–61). Their lifestyle has also provided the inspiration for a private treehouse complex in Oxfordshire.

Ewok Village was commissioned as a secret Christmas present in 2001. Mrs Taylor asked John Harris, one of Britain's most prolific treehouse designers, to create an elevated play area for her two young daughters. She hoped that a woodland village would be a magical place where her girls could play.

The site lies deep at the bottom of an Oxfordshire estate. The ten-minute walk from the large house takes you through the formal gardens, past the gypsy caravan, and into an untamed wood of free-seeded beech. Stay on the path and you will reach a stagnant pond covered in a film of green slime, adding to the unearthly Ewok atmosphere. Once you are there look up the steep hill and you will see three curvaceous treehouses linked together by a web of ladders and suspended rope bridges.

The £20,000 complex was built over the space of nine autumn weeks in 2001. Three teams of professional treehouse builders designed one each. The largest, which includes bunk beds and furnishings, has an area of eighteen square metres. The smallest is eight square metres. All are built of beech, in harmony with the surroundings.

Much like the original Ewok village, secrecy and defence are key considerations. There are countless exits and access points to the treehouses. On one deck there is a zip slide allowing occupants to whiz across the pond and land safely on the other side.

Although Ewok Village makes a perfect summer party venue, the treehouses are principally used as playrooms. They are not heated, nor connected to any electrical supply as that would have gone against the Ewoks' back-to-nature life choice. Instead they are used whenever weather permits.

Like all treehouses, Ewok Village is constantly evolving. At the time of writing there were plans to suspend a long swing on a tree further up the hill.

LEFT The private complex of three play treehouses was inspired by the Ewoks, stars of *Return of the Jedi*.

PRINCES' PLAYHOUSE

HIGHGROVE GLOUCESTERSHIRE, ENGLAND

LEFT Architect William Bertram took aesthetic inspiration from the host holly tree.

ABOVE The treehouse in its new position in the stumpery.

In 1987 HRH The Prince of Wales commissioned architect William Bertram to design a treehouse for his sons. It was one of several features destined for an overgrown corner of Highgrove, the Gloucestershire estate that Prince Charles has been cultivating to great acclaim since the early 1980s.

Soon afterwards Bertram, Prince Charles, and a young Prince William wandered into a copse outside the Kitchen Garden wall. Hidden within the overgrowth were some old sycamore and holly trees. One of the latter was selected for the treehouse.

The star-shaped platform, four metres up in the tree, was built by a local craftsman, David Palmer. Then Bertram got to work. His design took aesthetic inspiration from the holly tree itself. The door and balustrades mimic the shape of the pointed leaves; red-fringed doorframes and handrails and a dark green balcony refer to the colours of the holly tree.

The small volume – just enough for two young boys – was topped by a Hobbit-style thatched roof, and ringed by a small balcony. The means of access was changed from a 'pole with broomstick handles' to a 'rustic' fixed staircase up to the platform. The original idea was considered too dangerous; the latter much more appropriate.

Of course, in dealing with the future King of England, safety was a prime consideration. Bertram's original design included a net, 'of the sort that one might find under a trapeze artist at a circus'. But it proved impractical. In the end the built scheme featured very few concessions to safety. 'I tried to retain the sense of danger. That's what children like.'

By the late 1990s the holly tree was showing signs of age, making the treehouse increasingly precarious. In 2002 it was relocated to the nearby 'stumpery' – an area of garden full of old tree stumps, creating the effect of an organic grotto. It now sits on slate pillars. During the relocation process it was re-thatched and comprehensively overhauled. Access is now up a short slate staircase.

It was in its current location that the three princes, Charles, William and Harry, posed for the photographer Mario Testino in 2003. The image featured on the Highgrove Christmas card that year.

AT WORK WITH NATURE

TREEHOUSE OFFICE PENTLAND HILLS, SCOTLAND

Treehouses are flexible. They can be used as spare bedrooms, play spaces for children, even school rooms. Increasingly they are being used as office space.

In 2002 Robert Wilson, chairman of a large homoeopathy company, commissioned the TreeHouse Company to design an office which would allow him to work from home without being disturbed by his young children. The structure, hidden amidst the Pentland Hills of Scotland, is both practical and a reflection of his values.

As chairman of a company with a great respect for the protection and nurture of plant life, Wilson insisted on the use of materials and construction techniques which would be sympathetic to the host sycamore tree. Timber used in the house is selected Canadian and Scandinavian redwood, purchased from recognized forestry companies which exceed all replanting requirements.

The elevated office also conforms to the widely held belief that breaking contact with the ground has healing properties. Inhabiting a place not walled in by concrete but made from nature's own resources is an excellent way of re-establishing ties to the earth. Others speak about the creative power that can be harnessed up in the trees.

The design is based on Wilson's brief for a fully equipped office that reflects the idea of a treehouse as a place of magic and adventure. Its bright red clapperboard cladding demands attention. A small chimney puffs smoke from the wood-burning stove below. French windows fold out on to the veranda, and a balcony runs along one side of the building.

Wilson also wanted to take advantage of the stunning views of the surrounding hills by having a large window where his desk would sit, so that he could look over the fields as he worked and watch the changing colours of the seasons.

At thirty square metres the platform is quite large. To support it without the use of support posts, knee bracers – triangular supports attached to the trunk underneath the base – were used and to spread the load steel wires fixed to extended platform joists were suspended from the top of the sycamore tree. 'Because it's such a mature tree we could have relied on the support cables on their own,' explains John Harris.

A two-tier fixed staircase offers access into the treehouse. The interior is clad with horizontal lining boards painted cream. Each window is unique; there is a nautical round window wrapped in coconut rope and a more classical arched window.

The office is equipped with all mod cons including a fridge and a sink for evening entertaining.

ABOVE All timber came from sustainable sources.

RIGHT The treehouse office reflects its owner's homoeopathic beliefs.

SUSPENDED SPHERICAL TREEHOUSES

'EVE' VANCOUVER ISLAND, CANADA

Engineer Tom Chudleigh originally planned to build a houseboat. He envisaged a large wooden sphere supported on a catamaran-like frame, but before getting down to work he decided to build a smaller prototype to iron out potential problems. And so was born the suspended treehouse sphere.

Work began in 1995. Four years later, on the cusp of the millennium, 'Eve' was hoisted into a small cedar grove near Chudleigh's Vancouver Island home.

The construction process, which borrows from nautical technology, was extremely laborious. To create a true sphere Chudleigh, who is an engineer with a background in boat building, first created a wooden skeleton, like a globe without a surface. The skeleton was composed of ten bent wood half circles, arching from pole to pole. These were kept in shape by a circular band, wrapped around the centre of the globe.

To create the surface Chudleigh glued two long laminations of thin yellow cedar strips. These were laid over the frame, and attached to the top and bottom of the skeleton. When complete the thin rigid shell was covered with two layers of woven fibreglass and set in epoxy. This gave the effect of a heavy coat of varnish, drawing out the grain and texture of the wood.

The interior is modelled on a yacht. There is a double bed under the metre-wide circular window and a sofa and table occupy the other end. Eve, who has a diameter of 2.7 metres, can accommodate three people comfortably. She is also wired for electricity, sound and telephone.

By autumn 1999 the dream of a houseboat was long forgotten. Instead of a life on the ocean waves Chudleigh had set his sights on immersion in the forest canopy.

The sphere was hung from ropes attached to three trees to distribute the load and create a stable hang. Although Eve bounces around when anyone moves inside, the movement in the wind is very gentle.

The original means of access was a stepladder followed by a courageous scramble through the door. Today a stylish Chudleigh-designed spiral staircase wraps around the trunk of the nearest tree. At the top a short suspension bridge leads visitors into the sphere. The bridge, staircase and sphere are all hung from ropes. Eve makes minimal impact on her environment.

LEFT Access is via a spiral staircase and short bridge.

ABOVE TOP The staircase wraps around the trunk of the nearest tree.

ABOVE The suspension bridge leads visitors into the sphere.

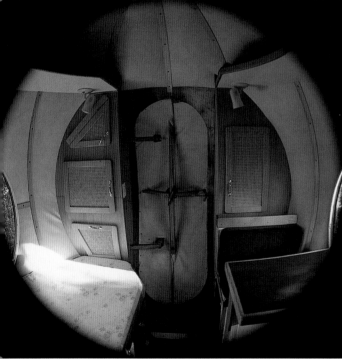

The sphere is easy to move around. A team of three can raise the treehouse into the branches in three days. A further three days are required for the staircase and suspension bridge. But it only takes a day to bring her down. For more remote locations there is nothing to stop the sphere being transported by helicopter. When empty it weighs only 205 kilos.

Although Eve is light there is no doubting her structural strength. During one attempt to hang her two of the three ropes came loose and she swung with some force into a nearby tree trunk. But she just bounced off, like a ping-pong ball.

Apart from its strength the spherical form has two additional benefits, one acoustic, the other medicinal. Chudleigh is a believer in the 'spirit realm'. It is his assertion that a true sphere reflects 'energy waves' from the source to a spot directly opposite the geographic centre of the sphere. If Chudleigh clicks his fingers on one side of the sphere, and positions his ears the same distance from the other side, it feels as if the sound is inside his head. 'From a healing point of view this is beneficial. All true healing involves getting in touch with yourself,' he says.

A sphere is also the ideal place to listen to music, true surround sound.

In 2001 Chudleigh began working on Eryn, sphere number two. 'Eve was a little flawed,' he says. The attachment points were not quite right, and with three people inside space was extremely limited. Eryn has a slightly wider diameter and is made of sitka spruce, a lighter wood that takes glue well.

Beyond Eryn the future for treehouse spheres looks bright. Chudleigh has completed a mould of Eryn from which he plans to mass produce fibreglass spheres. Eve and Eryn each cost US$60,000–68,000. Chudleigh would like the fibreglass version to be less than a quarter of that price.

Looking even further into the future Chudleigh hopes to build a colony of ten tree spheres and hang them in dense old-growth forest. There would be a bathroom sphere, a kitchen sphere and enough space for twenty to thirty residents. 'There's something magical about the forest,' says Chudleigh. 'Up in the trees you see life from a different perspective.'

TOP LEFT Eve is wired for electricity, sound and telephone.

LEFT The interior is modelled on a yacht.

RIGHT Ropes distribute the load and create a stable hang.

MAGICAL MYSTERY

THE LINDI TREEHOUSE BLACK MOUNTAINS, WALES

A good treehouse designer lets the tree dictate shape and size. At this children's playhouse in Wales, a fork in the trunk created the opportunity for an entrance between the boughs. This in turn influenced the decision to create a platform on one side of the magnificent 300-year-old beech tree and the treehouse on the other. Visitors walk from the platform, down three steps in the boughs, and then into the treehouse itself. This creates the illusion of walking right into the tree.

The playhouse was designed by John Harris of the TreeHouse Company. He regards it as one of his finest, no small claim given that he has designed over 500 during his career.

In the mid 1990s Harris was originally approached by Mrs Price, the lady of the house, who had seen an article about treehouses in the *Sunday Times*. She asked Harris to design, 'a small building that you might imagine an animal living in'. For generations the Price estate, home to black swans and small ponies, has been famous for wildlife, and not all of it real. All young visitors are told tales about the tiger that lives under the rose bush, and the bear that lives in the wood.

After a number of meetings the phone went quiet. Harris assumed that the idea had been forgotten. A year later he was contacted by Sophie Price, who explained that her mother had died. The family had decided to commission the treehouse as a memorial. 'She told me that it wasn't to be too grand or sophisticated, but something close to the spirit of what a treehouse should be all about,' Harris recalls. Its official name is the 'Lindi Treehouse'.

Access to the platform is via both a rope ladder and fixed steps. At the top a timber balustrade ensures there are no mishaps. The platform, shielded by the tree from the main house, overlooks a small lake. The interior of the treehouse is clad in pine. It includes a bed and a light, airy play space.

Even today, several years after completion, it remains a magical place, well-used by all members of the family. An unusual grey/green stain adds to the air of mystery. John Harris is delighted: 'It changes constantly, in time with the seasons.'

LEFT The brief called for a 'small building that you might imagine an animal living in'.

FEASTING IN THE SKY

DINING ROOM BERWICK, ENGLAND

ABOVE The treehouse is fitted to a very high specification.

RIGHT The circular platform is built around seven branches.

When John Harris was approached to design this treehouse, Mrs Tullock told him it was a secret birthday present. Construction would have to take place between 9am and 5pm on weekdays, while her sons were away. There could be no mess, no evidence to give the game away.

A few weeks later Mrs Tullock said she had an admission to make. The treehouse was actually for her. She had insisted on the veil of secrecy because her husband knew nothing about it. 'All of a sudden I was extremely nervous,' said Harris. 'The pressure to keep things secret was one thing. But building a treehouse without the co-owner's consent was quite another.'

It seems that the pressure also told on Mrs Tullock. The evening before construction was due to begin she confessed to her husband. Harris recalls what he then learnt. 'She told me, "I'm sure he'll love it, it's just that he's not sure about it". It was not convincing, but I was glad the pressure was off.'

The brief was largely unaffected by the unusual turn of events. Regardless of the end-user, the client still wanted to spend the budget of around £35,000 for a large, circular treehouse with a fixed spiral staircase. It was to be finished to the highest specifications, with built-in audio equipment, and a hidden television. It was also fitted with plumbing, electricity, a kitchen, and double glazing.

The treehouse occupies a 200-year-old oak tree set within a large formal garden. The platform is built around seven branches. A further two go through the veranda. It was a very complicated build, due largely to the strong 'sail effect'. The estate is near Berwick, at the eastern end of the England/Scotland border. Throughout the year fierce winds blow off the North Sea, barely two miles away, and batter the Tullocks' estate. To accommodate movement in the wind the branches were fitted with sliders, brackets that allow the branches to move independently.

Since completion the treehouse has been used primarily as a dining room, although during the summer months it does provide a good vantage point from which to watch the tennis below.

For Mrs Tullock the biggest question has always been, what does my husband think? 'Well, when he's showing guests around, he now introduces it as "my treehouse". So I suppose that must be a good sign.'

CRADLED ALOFT

PORTALEDGES AND TREEBOAT HAMMOCKS

For recreational tree climbers with an urge to sleep in the canopy there are a number of options on the market. Perhaps the best known are the portaledge and the Treeboat Hammock.

The former, which requires only one point of attachment, is composed of a lightweight metal frame, with super-strength fabric base. Additional features include wraparound tent-like enclosures, carry bags, and of course safety harnesses. Treeboat Hammocks are unique to tree climbing and installed with two, three or four points of attachment, which gives them good stability and offers opportunities for 'creative rigging' in the branches. They are also much the cheaper option: a basic Treeboat costs around US$200 compared with around US$500 for a portaledge.

Sophia Sparks of New Tribe, a specialist tree-climbing equipment company based in Oregon, says they came up with the Treeboat 'because getting up into the top of a tree is only half the fun; the other half is getting to stay there, in blissful comfort'. Those in the know debate the relative merits of the two approaches. Andrew Taylor, a California-based arborist and amateur tree and rock climber, favours portaledges. 'They work well in trees. Because a portaledge is a single point system, it can be rigged almost anywhere in a tree.' Options include positioning it out on a large horizontal limb, leaving the portaledge hanging free. 'If you are concerned about the strength of the limb, a short section of rope can be used as a tensioned back-tie or guy,' says Taylor.

The portaledge can also be suspended directly from the trunk of the tree, which will result in one side rubbing against it – this is why portaledges are designed with one side reinforced.

'Access is quite straightforward,' adds Taylor. 'It's like climbing into a canoe. You are stepping from a firm base into something that is floating. But a safety harness must be worn at all times.' For anyone 'caught short' during the night, this can prove complicated, as Taylor found when he spent the night with his young son in a twin portaledge.

The idea is relatively new to tree climbing. Portaledges evolved from Big Wall climbing, an extreme sport with its origins in 1950s California. Yosemite Valley is known for its dramatic vertical and overhanging cliff faces, some over 3000 feet high. Walls this big cannot be climbed in a day. In those days climbers would sleep on ledges, sometimes only a foot wide. 'The advent of the portaledge made it possible, even relatively comfortable, to climb multi-day routes with no natural bivouac sites, and to survive being pinned to the wall in bad weather, sometimes for days at a time,' says Taylor.

The earliest portaledge is thought to have been made during the 1980s by climber Mike Graham – it was effectively a collapsible cot. The technology has come a long way since then. There is now even a camouflage model, especially for tree climbers.

LEFT Portaledges suspended near Mendocino on the Californian coast. Portaledges can be rigged almost anywhere in a tree.

TREEHOUSES OF THE FUTURE

INTERNATIONAL TREEHOUSE COMPETITION

CHINA, HAWAII, VIETNAM AND FIJI

The world's only known design competition for treehouses was launched in the year 2000. David Greenberg, head of Treehouses of Hawaii Inc, came up with the idea. He had won contracts to build treehouse resorts on four beaches around the Pacific Rim. But with neither the time nor expertise to design the combined total of around one hundred treehouses, Greenberg challenged the international architecture community to tackle the task.

The exotic and novel premise provoked a deluge of design innovation. More than 500 architects from 46 countries put forward ideas. Some were structurally feasible. Disappointingly, political and diplomatic pressures mean that the treehouse resorts have yet to be realized. But while negotiations are ongoing, and Greenberg's contracts remain valid, all is not lost.

The story began in the mid 1990s, when Greenberg, a Californian architecture graduate, relocated to Hawaii in search of a fresh career direction. Taking the opportunity to indulge a childhood passion, he set about building a treehouse on the Hawaiian island of Maui. The experience led to the formation of Treehouses of Hawaii, a company that builds and manages treehouse resorts.

For the next three years Greenberg searched for work. He found an ally in the State of Hawaii, particularly the Department of Business Economic Development and Tourism (DBEDT). In the late 1990s China was beginning to thaw towards the West. The Clinton administration was busy cultivating economic and political ties. Greenberg was a beneficiary of the *détente*.

'The DBEDT set me up with joint development partners in China and Vietnam, through a Governors Mission to sister cities,' says Greenberg. Fortunately for him China's Hainan Island is the sister province to Hawaii, enabling the US Department of Trade and Commerce to facilitate a mutually productive business arrangement. Greenberg was commissioned to design a masterplan for a treehouse resort at Boao Aquapolis, a 26 square mile tourist development. The Department also assisted with a similar approach in Hue Province, Vietnam. By early 2000 he had also secured contracts for Naviti Island, Fiji and a site in Hawaii.

The idea for the competition came from Frank Gehry's seventieth birthday party in Brentwood, California. Gehry's famous design for the Bilbao Guggenheim has been credited with regenerating the ailing Basque port. Among the guests on that day in February 1999 were Greenberg and Kiki Kiser, a friend trying to establish 'arcspace', an architecture web site. 'I went there to ask Gehry to design a treehouse in China,' says Greenberg. 'He agreed, but never did it.' So he and Kiser combined forces, deciding to run a competition for designs on the nascent site. 'The power of the internet with a good idea is amazing,' says Greenberg.

The competition brief called for self-contained treehouse apartments that were ecologically responsible, typhoon resistant and suitable for construction in coconut palms. Entries were required to accommodate two to six occupants, over 45–90 square metres. Construction specifications included the use of stainless steel sleeves to attach the houses to the trees and the application of locally sourced materials. Designers were also encouraged to integrate independent power supplies and combustible toilets. True to purist treehouse tradition, no structural elements were allowed to touch the ground. Few palms can support a treehouse wrapped around its trunk – most entries were for suspended structures.

The combined characteristics of palm trees (extremely bendy) and geographic conditions (prone to monsoon rains and high winds) also dictated the nature of the submissions. High treehouses and rigid anchors were discouraged. Palm trees can reach heights of over 12 metres. Serious winds can blow them in all directions. Inflexible treehouses would be ripped apart.

In January 2001 Greenberg and an 11-strong jury whittled the 500 entries down to 100 commended schemes. Four overall winners were voted by the designers of the commended schemes. There were two German teams, a Swiss duo, and a US/Irish joint entry. All were ready to get started. But almost immediately a sequence of incapacitating bad luck began.

In fact the sequence predates the selection of winning designs. In May 2000 George Speight led a coup to overthrow the Fijian government, creating an inclement climate for commerce, and all but decimating the tourist industry. Greenberg's plans were shelved, though perhaps not permanently. In April 2001 a US naval surveillance plane collided with a Chinese jet near Hainan, leading to allegations of spying. The event dealt a blow to Sino-American diplomatic relations. Greenberg's plans for Hainan were placed on hold. They still are.

The next major event with implications for Greenberg's treehouses was the 11 September 2001 terrorist attack on the World Trade Center, New York. The Bali bombing of October 2002 compounded the catastrophe. And then, in April 2003, SARS struck. Global pandemonium followed China's admission that a serious virus, with symptoms similar to influenza, was spreading through South-East Asia and Canada. The outbreak was controlled relatively quickly, but the tourist trade suffered another blow.

For Greenberg and his ambitious plans, the future is uncertain. But the response to the competition, and the fact that it was run at all, suggests that a beach-side treehouse resort will eventually be built somewhere on the Pacific Rim.

RIGHT The four winners (see over for details). **PREVIOUS PAGE** Experimental treehouse by Softroom (see page 157).

JENS KOLB, MARIANNE BAER & PETER DORR GERMANY

Coconuts thrive in costal conditions around the Pacific Rim. Evolution has perfected a strong multi-layered protective shell, capable of withstanding strong winds. With this in mind, the German team of Jens Kolb, Marianne Baer and Peter Dorr, designed two concept treehouses. One is distinctly esoteric, the other eminently buildable.

Initially the architects envisaged a 'treehouse in a bottle', a rugged coconut-shaped balloon that would compress into a small portable bottle. In theory the balloon could be inflated anywhere. All that would be required were trees, and the architects' 'bottle' complete with miniature pumping device. 'We hoped it could be a sort of rescue pack for areas struck by earthquake, for instance', say Kolb, Baer and Dorr.

It sounded great, but a scratch beneath the surface reveals the idea to be completely fantastical. There is no known material that can pack down to the required size. And inflation units required for such volumes are very large, and unlikely to be found on isolated Pacific Rim beaches. So the design trio went back to the drawing board.

The second scheme is a more literal interpretation of a coconut. Analysis of the nut reveals that its soft fleshy interior is protected by an inner load-bearing film and wrapped in a protective cocoon. Kolb, Baer and Dorr have applied this model to their treehouse. The living space is protected by wooden casing, designed with nautical technology. An outer shell of strong translucent material envelops the sphere for additional strength.

If built, the coconut treehouse would be strung between two or three palms, rolling around in the wind. To enhance the impression that the treehouse is floating, there would be minimal contact with the ground – perhaps only a rope would offer access and function as an anchor.

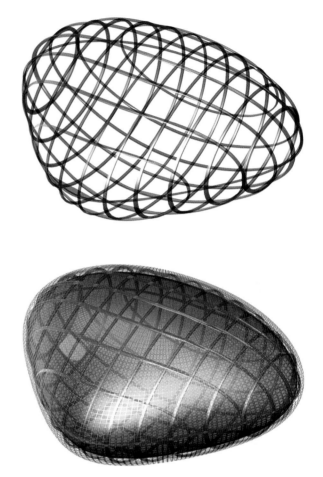

LEFT The pods are designed to be strung between palm trees.

RIGHT The design was inspired by coconuts, whose inner load-bearing film is wrapped in a protective cocoon.

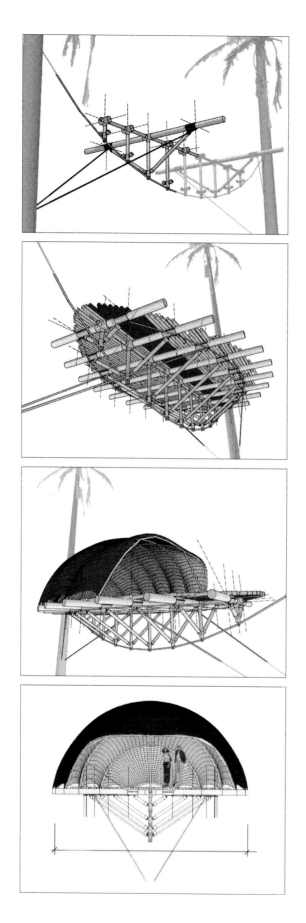

KENDEL ARCHITEKTEN GERMANY

Flexibility is the principal attribute of Kendel Architekten's 'lonesome nest', one of the four overall winners of David Greenberg's international architecture competition.

The hammock-like structure is supported by a wooden lattice grid-shell suspended on a stainless steel cable. It can accommodate anything from a single room to a family apartment. Distance between palm trees and the width of the trunk dictate the scale.

In theory, all that is required to build the treehouse are two palm trees, four metal joint modules, and a length of stainless steel cable. Two metal joint modules, one to take the strain, the other to act as anchor, attach the timber hammock to each tree. Interior design depends on available materials. Palm leaves or coco fibre mats can line the walls and floor, while waterproof and wind resistant parachute fabric acts as a roof.

The treehouse can be built in isolation, or in a small cluster radiating from a strong central palm. It was designed by Kendel Architekten, a family architecture practice based in Berlin.

Kendel Architekten has received some interest in their treehouse from a Venezuelan tour operator. But at the time of writing, the Venezuelans were waiting for a more robust tourist industry.

LEFT Stainless steel cables carry the weight of the treehouse.

TOP RIGHT A colony of 'lonesome nests'.

RIGHT The timber hammock supported by two palms.

MIREILLE TURIN & PETER SIGRIST SWITZERLAND

An inverse umbrella was the inspiration for Turin & Sigrist's tent-style kit treehouse, another of the four overall winners.

To erect the structure a stainless steel sleeve is attached to the trunk, around three metres from the ground. The tightly packed light metal frame is then unfurled and clad in weather resistant fabric, similar to the material used for catamaran decking. Once assembled a pulley system is used to haul the volume into place.

The weight of the treehouse is carried by the steel sleeve, which is firmly secured to the tree once the tent is airborne. Guy ropes anchor the treehouse to the ground. Its bulb-like form is streamlined to avoid buffeting in heavy winds.

The oval-shaped inverse umbrella fans out to create the floor, approximately two metres from the beach below. Inflatable cushions have been installed in the bottom of the fabric cloak to create a comfortable sleeping area.

Curtains subdivide the circular floorplan, providing flexible space for a maximum of four occupants. A double-layered canvas can be used to control ventilation.

The entrance is a round hole cut into the base. A rope ladder provides the only means of ascent.

Cooking and shower facilities are arranged around the tree trunk, shaded from the sun by the treehouse above. The shower damps down the ground, stopping sand blowing inside.

BELOW The weight of the tent-like treehouses is carried by a steel sleeve attached to the palm trunk.

BOTTOM The bulb-like forms are streamlined to minimize the buffeting in high winds.

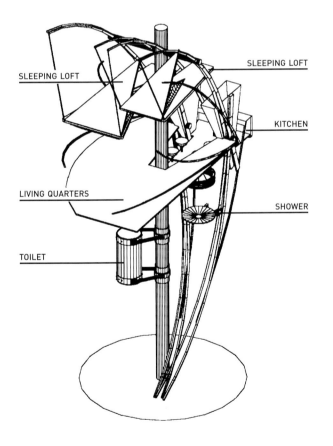

SLEEPING LOFT

SLEEPING LOFT

KITCHEN

LIVING QUARTERS

SHOWER

TOILET

FIELD LINES ARCHITECTURE USA

The treehouse competition was just a starting point for Field Lines. Since 2001 Marc Ackerson and Oisin Clancy have worked with engineers and yacht manufacturers to develop a kit treehouse for mass production.

They have named the project a.loft, which is described as 'a light, demountable, pre-engineered, fully equipped and vertically organised leisure accommodation'. At the time of writing a scale model, which fits into a small backpack, was due for laboratory testing.

As far as possible, a.loft has been inspired by natural forms. Animal movement and plant flexibility have been refined to use the minimum amount of matter for maximum effect. 'We have studied the aerodynamics of a bird's wing in flight, the aqua dynamic properties of a trout's tail, and even the characteristics of an elephant's skin', say Ackerson and Clancy. 'Like a leaf, a.loft has a curved spine, a soft body and delicate skin.'

The depth of research has also led to an extremely innovative method of attaching the treehouse to the tree. No metal insertions are required to pierce the trunk. Instead the treehouse is held in elastic tension, like a bow prior to the release of an arrow. Compressible mesh and foam are wrapped around the base of the trunk to anchor the house and protect the tree. The volume is supported by pneumatic clasps and controlled pressure created by clean air technology compressors. 'This means that the relationship between the tree and a.loft is symbiotic, not parasitical,' say the architects.

MODULAR DESIGN

EXPERIMENTAL TREEHOUSE SOFTROOM, UK

When Wallpaper* magazine commissioned the London architectural practice Softroom to design a concept treehouse the brief was a single word, 'Treehouse'. Christopher Bagot and Oliver Salway's response was a lightweight kit-of-parts designed to attach to a tree with minimal impact.

The treehouse is supported by a three-tier frame which is hoisted into place by crane. It is attached by a collar which is bolted through the trunk. With two punctures through the bark, the collar avoids excessive puncturing of the cambium layer, the tree's living membrane (see page 162).

The framework supports a range of drop-in components, including a toilet capsule, kitchen, storage units, and sleeping cradle. For safety a large net is stretched on structural booms around the perimeter. Access is via a metal ladder that can be retracted for security.

There are any number of optional extras. A secondary collar around the trunk will support a canopy and projecting arm, to which a shower hose or lamp can be attached. Depending on the extent of your ambition, cooking facilities, including a calor gas stove and a cool box, are concealed beneath hatches inside the kitchen table.

The treehouse was always intended to be an experiment. 'It was developed extremely quickly, so we took certain liberties with regards to structural analysis and construction,' explain the designers. They believe that with the proper resources there is no reason why the idea, or something similar, could not be built.

LEFT Softroom's experimental treehouse is a lightweight kit-of-parts.

TOP RIGHT The metal ladder can be retracted for security.

CENTRE RIGHT AND BOTTOM A secondary collar will support a canopy and projecting arm.

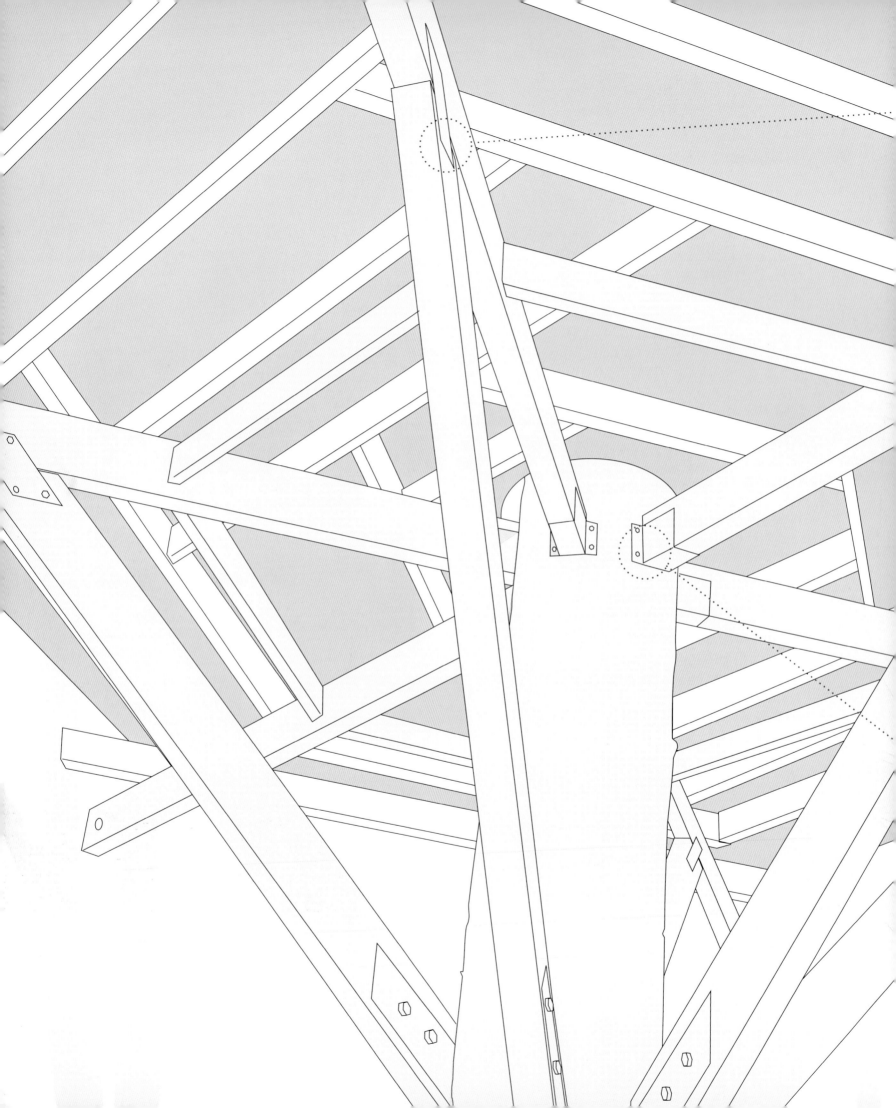

BUILDING A TREEHOUSE
PRACTICAL CONSIDERATIONS

There is no formula to treehouse construction. All trees have different shapes and identities. Location and climatic conditions are equally variable. But some general principles do apply.

PLANNING CONSENT

Rules and regulations differ according to global context, but as a rule of thumb if your treehouse is a full-time dwelling it will need to conform to local planning regulations. Most basic treehouses, without plumbing or electricity, will be free of constraints. But there are exceptions. Before building it is important to research local guidelines, especially if your treehouse overlooks another property, is particularly high, or might conceivably distract passing motorists. You must also find out whether your tree is protected by a preservation order. This will not necessarily preclude construction, but it may limit your options.

It is rare for a planning authority to create a scene about a treehouse, perhaps for fear of a public relations disaster. There are of course cautionary tales, like that of the treehouse specialist Patrick Fulton who was ordered to demolish his eight-year-old treehouse in Northern Ireland because it was built without consent. But even when consent is sought retrospectively, as was the case for Sam Edwards' treehouse in Georgia, USA (see pages 122–127), novelty value and sweet talk can often be used to your advantage. Many planning officers will never have come across a treehouse before.

For insurance purposes most treehouses are treated as outhouses. Premiums may be increased for elaborate treehouses to reflect rebuilding costs in the event of storm or fire damage.

CHOOSING YOUR TREE

The choice of tree will dictate the longevity, shape and height of your treehouse. It will also have bearing on ease of access, and the seasonal availability of daylight.

Most of the world's more durable treehouses sit in healthy mature hardwoods. Good host trees include oak, fir, maple, beech, ash and willow. Regardless of species, experts recommend that load-bearing branches have a minimum diameter of 17.5cm. Look out for trees whose branches begin to radiate horizontally at around 3–6m from the ground, like the fingers of an upturned hand. These are ideal for treehouses that sit in the palm, providing 360 degree support and views.

The search for the perfect tree is almost certainly futile. Keep an eye out for groups of trees – there is no limit on numbers – whose composite strength and orientation can provide support. In some cases pruning will be required to create space for a treehouse and to lighten the tree's load. It may look easy, but this is a skilled job. Search out a local tree surgeon or arborist.

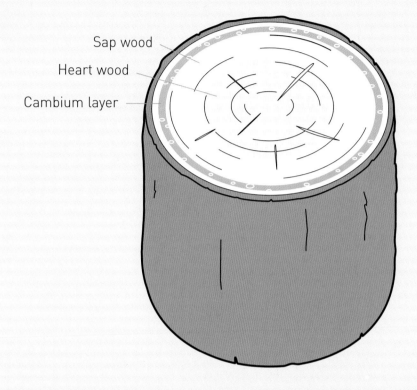

Sap wood

Heart wood

Cambium layer

STRONG, HEALTHY ATTACHMENTS

Perhaps the most hotly debated aspect of treehouse construction is the impact upon the host tree. Experienced purists resist all temptation to insert any kind of metal bolt into the tree, preferring to rely on cables and other non-intrusive attachments. On the opposite end of the spectrum, first time builders with limited knowledge of trees often err on the side of safety, using five nails where one would do. The ideal approach is somewhere in between.

Like humans, trees have a natural capacity for self-healing. From a tree's perspective small metal insertions create wounds, which it clots with sap. There are ways of minimizing the damage, but a bolt or nail will not be fatal. Lacerating or strangling the cambium layer will be.

The cambium layer is the tree's living membrane – the dead core of a tree provides structural support. Protected by the bark, the cambium layer is a network of tubes that feeds the tree. It is the arboreal equivalent of a blood supply. If it is cut even half the way round the tree will die. Misuse of

ropes and pulleys can be equally cataclysmic. To avoid strangulation wrap a layer of non-perishable material around the trunk or branch.

It is preferable to use bolts and nails of galvanized steel to avoid rusting, which can stain and even poison some trees. Aim to make a small number of bolts go a long way, so consider strategic placement to optimize loads. Use long bolts – aside from puncturing the cambium layer, there will be no danger to the tree's health. And avoid placing bolts or nails close to each other. The tree may interpret a cluster of insertions as one wound, killing the area in between.

Apart from metal insertions the main types of attachment include cables (rope and steel) and metal braces wrapped around the trunk. Cables are commonly used on multi-tree structures, because they have the flexibility to accommodate natural movement. Metal braces provide a solid base in instances where the trunk offers the sole means of attachment.

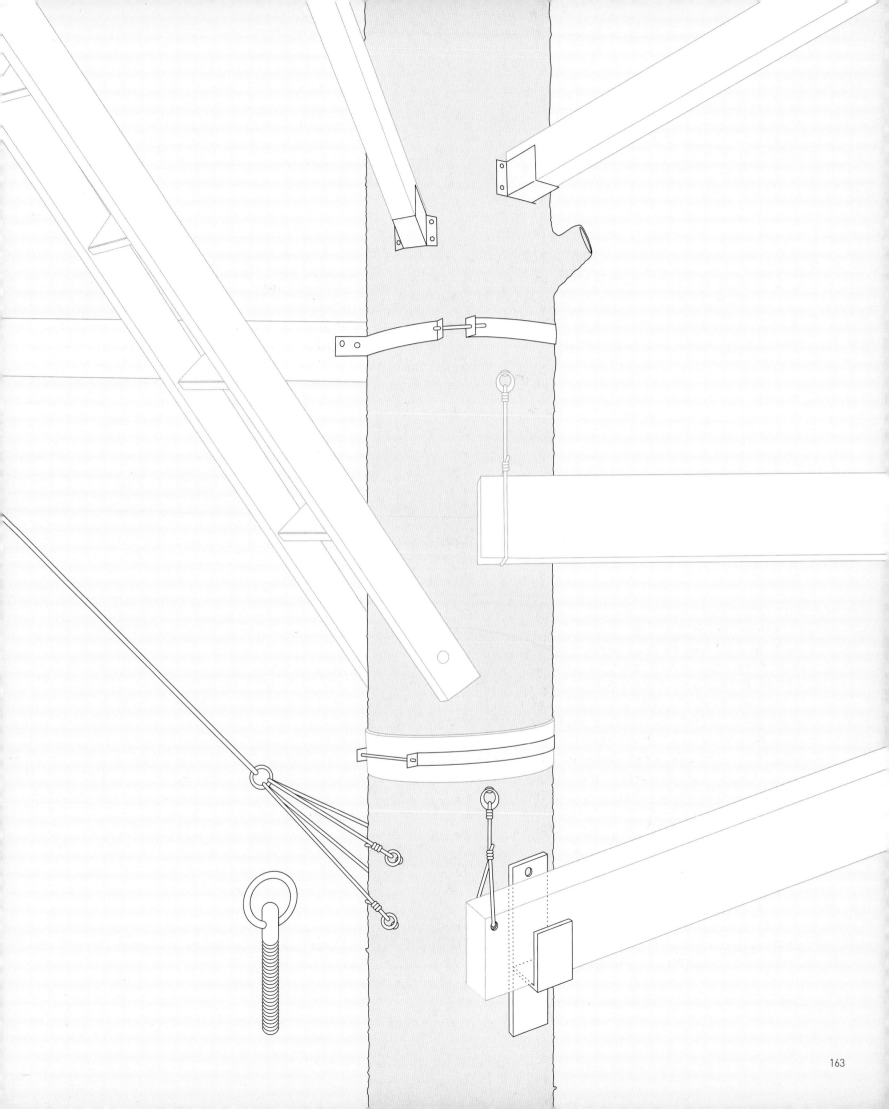

DESIGN AND BUILD

When it comes to design, be guided by your host. The shape of the tree, its location, neighbours and age all have a bearing on the finished product. That said there must also be elements of planning. Very few successful treehouses simply evolve. Even if your plans extend no further than a sketch on an envelope, it will at least give you a sense of proportion, materials and points of access.

A treehouse is as durable as its base. With a strong platform anything is possible, from the addition of a roof, to further storeys. Experts recommend building your base in the bottom eighth of the tree – the lower the treehouse the greater its strength and centre of gravity. Keeping it low will also reduce the 'sail effect', where the treehouse bulk increases the wind load.

Most strong platforms are built as close to the trunk as possible. If building as if in the palm of an upturned hand (see Choosing your tree), first arrange four beams over available branches, using a spirit level to ensure they are level. A uniform rectangle with 90 degree corners is the ideal scenario, but rarely realistic. Once secured with deep bolts and supporting nails, add horizontal beams over the top. If the shape of the tree allows, place diagonal bracing below the platform for added strength.

For multi-tree structures, or treehouses with one or more sides supported on poles, the manipulation and management of the platform becomes easier. On the other hand, increased tree numbers makes the accommodation of wind movement more complex, and may require use of cables or sliding joints for flexible support (see Strong, healthy attachments).

For complex treehouses, like those built around the trunk with a platform supported by cantilevered beams, metal brackets and support braces must be used. This is best left to the experts.

Once the platform is in place it is time to add walls and a roof. The options are endless. But as far as possible put the treehouse together on the ground and hoist it into place. Mid-air construction is dangerous and difficult. After construction is complete, the pulley can be used to hoist provisions, and sometimes even people.

MATERIALS

The vast majority of treehouses are built of wood. It is widely available, lightweight and aesthetically sympathetic.

As the examples in the book demonstrate, there are many options as to the kind of wood. Typical choices include high quality oak beams for the base, factory-finished tongue-and-groove floorboards, and treated plywood boards as walls. But personal preference and regional availability also have a bearing. Some people try to use salvaged wood, which can be particularly useful for doors and window frames.

A common exception to the wood only approach is the roof. Corrugated iron is a global favourite. It is water resistant, inexpensive and reasonably light. But it is far from the only option. You might consider creating a roof frame of wooden battens, and covering it with a tarpaulin, leaves, plywood panels or roofing felt.

Finally, it might seem obvious, but keep all materials and contents as light as possible.

ACCESS

Pulling up a rope ladder to keep intruders out conforms to the romantic image of the treehouse as a private bolthole, but rope ladders are not easy to climb. Fixed points of access are much more common. Although a wooden ladder fixed to the ground is not exotic, the easy life is a preference for many. Fixed ladders are also simple to maintain and safe to use. Handrails are a strongly recommended accessory.

Arguably the most elegant and certainly the most space efficient means of access is the spiral staircase. Curling gracefully around the trunk of a tree the spiral ascends to the sky in suitably disorientating style. But they are complicated to build. It is preferable for the spiral to be independent of the tree, using the trunk only to lean on. Individual steps supported by the trunk require multiple insertions through the cambium layer and it is difficult to ensure their strength. Stand-alone spiral staircases are another option, but can look a little contrived by comparison.

To some extent the means of access depends on the height of the treehouse. The majority have fixed points of access because the majority are close to the ground. For higher treehouses a sequence of ladders linked to small platforms, rope pulleys, and even a water-powered lift (see Kerala Green Magic, page 88) are viable alternatives.

Another consideration is how to enter the treehouse. Will the ladder or pulley be on the edge of the treehouse, or will you build a trapdoor in the base?

SAFETY AND MAINTENANCE

If properly maintained a treehouse can last for several years, not just a summer. To achieve longevity regular inspections of all structural elements and load bearing branches should become a ritual. Monitoring the condition of the platform and ropes are also basic commonsense measures for all treehouses regardless of their distance from the ground. But nothing has greater relevance to the long term well-being of a treehouse than the health of the tree it sits in.

Trees are generally resilient plants, but they are exposed and distinctly vulnerable. To flourish they need nourishment and respect. And they are also in a perpetual state of evolution, losing limbs, growing new ones, and expanding at the girth. Almost all professional treehouse builders will offer regular check-ups on your treehouse to ensure that the tree has room to expand around the treehouse. But constant self-assessment is vital.

THE COST OF A TREEHOUSE

You are unlikely to build a durable treehouse for less than £2,000/US$3,300. This fee assumes high quality materials and professional assistance – from a treehouse specialist, tree surgeon, planning advisor and so on. We have listed some treehouse building specialists on page 171.

This image demonstrates what not to do when building a treehouse. Unless positioned on a stump, all treehouses should be built in live, healthy trees, and power cables must be secured out of harm's way. To avoid the need for planning consent, build well away from roads, and do not overlook other dwellings (see page 161).

BIBLIOGRAPHY

Aikman, Anthony, *Treehouses*, Robert Hale, London, 1988.

Audot, L., *Traité de la composition et de l'ornement des jardins*, 2 vols, 6th edition, 1859.

Creasey, Brian, 'Peto Tree House at Easton Lodge', *Garden History Society News* 62, Summer 2001, p.29.

d'Esnambuc, Pierre Blain, *Le Gros Chene – Son Histoires, Ses Gloires*, new edition, Ph Vallée – R. Bourdon, Auffay, France, 1993.

Humphreys, Phebe Westcott, *The Practical Book of Garden Architecture*, J.B.Lippincott, Philadelphia and London, 1914.

Ingpen, Robert, *The Afternoon Treehouse*, Pavilion Books Ltd, London, 1997.

Lazzaro, Claudia, *The Italian Renaissance Garden: from the conventions of planting, design, and ornament to the grand gardens of sixteenth-century central Italy*, Yale University Press, New Haven and London, 1990.

Matthiessen, Peter, *The tree where man was born*, Picador, London, 1972.

Mitton, Robert, *The Lost World of Irian Jaya*, Oxford University Press, Melbourne, 1983.

Muller, Kal, *Indonesian New Guinea – Irian Jaya*, Periplus Editions, Berkeley, California, 1991.

Mungazi, Dickson A., *Gathering under the mango tree – values in traditional culture in Africa*, American University Studies, New York, 1996.

Nelson, Peter, *Treehouses, the art and craft of living out on a limb*, Houghton Mifflin Company, New York, 1994.

Nelson, Peter; Nelson, Judy, and Larkin, David, *The Treehouse Book*, Universe Publishing, New York, 2000.

Oliver, Paul, *Dwellings*, Phaidon, London, 2003.

Pearson, David, *Treehouses – The house that Jack built*, Gaia Books, London, 2001.

Petit, Victor, *Habitations champêtres – Recueil de maisons, villas, chalets, pavilions, kiosques, berceaux, parterres, gazons, serres, orangeries, parcs et jardins*, 1855.

Plinius Secundus (Caius) [Pliny the Elder], *The Natural History of Pliny*, trans. J. Bostock and H. T. Riley, 6 vols, London, 1857.

Politzer, Annie and Michel, *Huts and tree houses*, Editions Gallimard, Paris, 1974.

Temple, Judith, 'Robinson: A rustic playground', *Garden History Society News* 60, Autumn 2000, pp.18-21.

Van Enk, Gerrit and de Vries, Lourens, *The Korowai of Irian Jaya, the language in its cultural context*, Oxford University Press, New York and Oxford, 1997.

Vieweg, Burkhard, *Muschelgeld und Sudseegeister, authentische berichte aus Deutsch-Neuguinea 1906-1909*, Verlag Josef Margraf, Germany, 1990.

Wilkinson, Elizabeth, *The House of Boughs: A Sourcebook for Garden Designs, Structures and Suppliers*, Penguin, Australia, 1985.

A SELECT LIST OF SPECIALIST TREEHOUSE BUILDERS AND CONSULTANTS

Free Spirit Spheres

Tom Chudleigh

342 E26 Ave
Vancouver, BC
VSV 2H5
Canada

E-mail: tomchud@dowco.com
Web: www.freespiritspheres.com

Patrick Fulton

Advice about all aspects of treehouse design and maintenance

Limavady
Northern Ireland
E-mail: treehouseguy@iname.com

Web: www.fulton.btinternet.co.uk & www.thetreehouseguide.com

Out 'n' About

Treesort & Treehouse Institute

300 Page Creek Road
Cave Junction, Oregon 97523
USA

E-mail: treesort@treehouses.com
Web: www.treehouses.com

TreeHouse Company

John Harris

The Stables
Maunsheugh Road
Fenwick
Scotland KA3 6AN

E-mail: info@treehouse-company.com
Web: www.treehouse-company.com

Treehouses of Hawaii

David Greenberg

E-mail: hanatreehouse@yahoo.com
Web: www.treehousesofhawaii.com

TreeHouse Workshop, Inc

Peter Nelson

2901 W Commodore Way
Seattle, WA 98199
USA

E-mail: jake@treehouseworkshop.com
Web: www.treehouseworkshop.com

CONTACT DETAILS FOR TREEHOUSES TO VISIT FEATURED IN THIS BOOK

Ackergill Tower by Wick
Caithness
Scotland KA1 4RG
E-mail: ruth@ackergill-tower.co.uk
Web: www.ackergill-tower.co.uk

The Treehouse at The Alnwick Garden
Alnwick
Northumberland
England NE66 1YU
E-mail: info@alnwickgarden.com
Web: www.alnwickgarden.com

Big Beach in the Sky
Island of Hainan
China
E-mail: hanatreehouse@yahoo.com
Web: www.treehousesofhawaii.com

Cedar Creek Treehouse
P.O. Box 204
Ashford
WA 98304
USA
E-mail: treehouse@mashell.com
Web: www.cedarcreektreehouse.com

Green Magic Treehouse Resort
Thalipuzha
Vythiri
Kerala
India
E-mail: greenmagic@hotelskerala.com
Web: www.hotelskerala.com/greenmagic

Hotell Hackspett
Västerås
Sweden
E-mail: info@mikaelgenberg.com
Web: www.mikaelgenberg.com

Treehouse Hotel
Green Iguana Sanctuary
Punta Uva
Costa Rica
E-mail: reservation@fostersroatan.com
Web: www.costaricatreehouse.com
Web: www.iguanaverde.com

West Bay Treehouse
Roatan
Honduras
Web: www.fostersroatan.com

Wilderness Treehouse Lodge
c/o Wm. Eric Schmidt
P.O. Box 110504
Anchorage
AK 99511-0504
USA
E-mail: info@akwild.com
Web: www.akwild.com

ACKNOWLEDGEMENTS

The authors and publisher would like to thank the following for their help in the preparation of this book:

Ahadu Abaineh, Marc Ackerson, Marianne Baer, William Bertram, Edsart Besier, Leslie Beverly, Marie-France Boyer, Gordon Brown, Susan Campbell, Tom Chudleigh, Oisin Clancy, Bill Compher, Richard Craven, Ingrid Crawford, Richard Crawley, Foster Diaz, Peter Dorr, Sam Edwards, Imogen Evans, Lynn Ferrante, Amanda Foster, Robert Garneau, Mikael Genberg, Lynne Goodwin, David Greenberg, Lode Greven, John Harris, Mary Henderson, Jan Kendel, Jens Kolb, Miko, V.K.Moorthy, The Duchess of Northumberland, Mirabel Osler, Eric Schmidt, Peter Sigrist, Sophia Sparks, George Steinmetz, Jean Stone, Andrew Taylor, Mireille Turin, Babu Varghese, Clare Wilks, Prokop Zavada and the staff of the British Library, the Print Room of the British Museum and the Lindley Library, Royal Horticultural Society.

PICTURE CREDITS

Ahadu Abaineh: 66, 67

© Nadine Agosti 2003: 136, 137, 138, 139

The Alnwick Garden: 108–9, 110, 111, 112–3

Bär, Kolb & Dörr: 149 below, 150, 151

Leslie Beverly: 98 below, 101

www.bridgeman.co.uk: 8–9 (Victoria & Albert Museum, London), 12 (British Museum, London), 14 above (Castello Sforzesco, Milan), 20 below, 21 (Fitzwilliam Museum, Cambridge), 25, 32–3 (Harris Museum and Art Gallery, Preston, Lancashire), 37

By permission of the British Library: 15 (Maps K. Top. 82:12, c-1), 27 above (Add. MS 78610C © The Evelyn Family, c/o Monkhouse and Bannisters)

© The Trustees of The British Museum: 22–3 (1948-4-10-4 (216) 1577.a.38), 31 (P.979 1856-6-7-7 Hollar vol. VIII)

By permission of the heirs of Jean de Brunhoff: 46–7

www.clarewilks.co.uk: 116, 117, 118, 119

Bill Compher (www.cedarcreektreehouse.com): 102, 103, 104, 105

Courtauld Institute of Art: 14 below

Richard Craven: 128, 129 (photographer Alex Ramsay)

Ingrid Crawford: 62, 64

© D. Donne Bryant Stock Photography Agency: 99, 100

Mary Evans Picture Library: 6

Field Lines Architecture, New York: 149 below centre, 155

Freer Gallery of Art, Smithsonian Institution, Washington, D.C.: 43 (Purchase, F1950.2)

The Gardens of Easton Lodge (www.eastonlodge.co.uk): 11, 38, 39

Mikael Genberg (www.mikaelgenberg.com): 94, 95, 96, 97

David Greenberg (www.treehousesofhawaii.com): 86, 87

Lode Greven/Free Lens Photography: 68–9, 74, 76–7, 78–9

Kendel Architekten: 149 above, 152, 153

© Gavin Kingcome: 81, 82, 83, 84, 85

Lucinda Lambton/arcaid.co.uk: 28–9

Andrew Lawson: 132, 133

Lothlorien art copyright The Brothers Hildebrandt All Rights Reserved: 48 (for information regarding original Hildebrandt Tolkien art and products go to http://www.spiderwebart.com or e-mail brothershildebrandt@spiderwebart.com)

© National Maritime Museum, London: 26

Private collection: 20 above, 20 centre, 27 centre, 27 below, 34, 35, 40–1, 42, 80, 98 above

© Louie Psihoyos: 51, 144–5

Royal Horticultural Society, Lindley Library: 36

Courtesy of the Arthur M. Sackler Museum, Harvard University Art Museums: 44 (Gift of John Goelet, formerly in the collection of Louis J. Cartier. Photo Katya Kalisen)

Scala, Florence: 16–7, 18–9, 24

Eric Schmidt: 70, 71, 73

Copyright E. H. Shepard: 49 (line illustration from WINNIE-THE-POOH by A.A. Milne, reproduced by permission of Curtis Brown Group Ltd., London and Atrium Verlag, Zürich 1987)

© Paul Shoffner: 114–5, 122–3, 124–5, 126–7

Softroom UK: 146–7, 156, 157

George Steinmetz/Katz Pictures Limited: 54–5, 56, 58–9, 60, 61

TreeHouse Company (www.treehouse-company.com), telephone +44 (0)1560 600111: 106, 107, 130–1, 134, 135, 140–1, 142, 143

Mireille Turin & Peter Sigrist: 149 above centre, 154

Shaun Walker//www.ottermedia.com: 65

Scott Wotherspoon: 2–3, 4, 158–169

Dave Young (www.daveyoung.co.uk): 52, 88, 89, 90, 91, 92, 93

Prokop Zavada: 121

INDEX

Frances Lincoln Ltd
4 Torriano Mews
Torriano Avenue
London NW5 2RZ
www.franceslincoln.com

British Library Cataloguing in Publication data
A catalogue record for this book is available from the British Library

First Frances Lincoln edition: 2005

ISBN 0 7112 2437 4

Printed and bound in Singapore by CS Graphics

9 8 7 6 5 4 3 2 1

Commissioned and edited by Jane Crawley
Designed by Caroline Clark
Picture editor Sue Gladstone